Front and back cover:
**Canopic jars of Padiouf**
The Louvre

Pages 2/3:
**Tomb of Sethos I in the Valley of the Kings**

Page 6:
**Tomb of Sethos I in the Valley of the Kings**

Page 8:
**The cat goddess Bastet**
The Louvre

Page 11:
**The bull god Apis**
The Louvre

Pages 112 and 129:
**Breast-plate representing Isis and Nephtys**
The Louvre


ISBN: 2.907670.32.8.
Printed in Italy

**Photographic credits:**

**R.M.N.**: 1, 8, 11, 13, 14/15, 19, 20/21, 27, 30/31, 33, 37, 42/43, 45, 46/47, 49, 50/51, 53, 55, 56/57, 59, 63, 68/69, 73, 75, 79, 80/81, 84, 89, 107, 108/109, 112, 129, 136.

**Jean de Beler**: 2/3, 6, 16/17, 23, 25, 39, 61, 65, 67, 77, 91, 93, 95, 97, 98/99, 101, 103, 111.

**Slide**/Bavaria: 35.
**Slide**/Hahn: 29.
**Slide**/Steffens: 40/41.

**Text:** A. Gros de Beler.
**Contribution:** F. Boutmy.

# EGYPTIAN MYTHOLOGY

Aude Gros de Beler

Foreword
Aly Maher el Sayed

# EGYPTIAN MYTHOLOGY

Aude Gros de Beler

Foreword
Aly Maher el Sayed

MOLIÈRE

# *FOREWORD*

The desire to understand Egyptian Mythology is often, irrespective of religious preference, part of a search for the source of our spirituality and for the light that has been throwing a particular glow on men's ambitions and metaphysical speculations for thousands of years.

That history was born on the banks of the Nile is common wisdom, but the fact that spirituality and religious concept also stem from there is less obvious; probably because we have false ideas that Egyptians were a polytheistic and zoolastic people.

So to enter the pantheon of ancient Egypt is to try and understand the complex relationships that united Gods to men; it is to try to reach, through multiple transpositions, half human, half beast, the divine nature that haunts all civilizations...

It is to go out to meet these deities that rule life and death, sky and earth, light and darkness, night and day, order and chaos... It is to apprehend these multiformed gods that all drift from abstractness to the search of the absolute... divinities, fabulous emanations of Re', the sun god, the substance of the soul of the earth and all beings looking for immortality.

This work is not a theological treatise, but a breviary; it contains more than fifty gods, and may give a conception of divinity that is not so different from ours... These gods are multiple and one at the same time, they might not represent the Truth, but a symbolical truth: if the ancient Egyptians built temples, pyramids and statues, it was because they had glimpsed the invisible through the visible; and if they wanted to preserve the corporal element, it was to make resurrection of the soul possible and to open the doors of eternity.

The philosophy on which this mythology is based can still be useful for our modern world; more than four thousand years later, it remains, on the eve of the third millennium, very true, and an important element in the search for wisdom and truth.

Aly MAHER EL SAYED
Egyptian Ambassador

# CONTENTS

# *Amun*

Amun 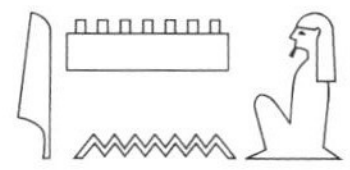

*Associated a in triad with the goddess Mut, and with a son, Khons*

*A solar god created in Thebes under the name of Amun Re', he became a dynastic god for the whole of Egypt under the Middle Kingdom*

*Principal place of worship: Karnak / Luxor (Upper Egypt)*

*Representation: a man crowned with two feathers*

The Egyptian texts describe him as *"the king of Gods."* However, if one is to judge from the mythological tales, nothing predestined this deity to have this status. In the Old Kingdom, ***Amun*** seems to have been relatively unknown, as the only mention of his name appears in the "**The Pyramid Texts**," the first inscription of which dates back to *Unas*, a pharaoh of the 5th Dynasty. In fact ***Amun***'s integration into the pantheon goes back to the Middle Kingdom. He appeared in **Thebes**, and progressively his cult began its ascendancy. Many attributes of other divine beings were conferred upon him, and he became, at the beginning of the 18th Dynasty, a state god, universal and creative.

The origin of ***Amun*** is quite mysterious. For some, he was one of the eight primeval gods of the cosmogony at **Hermopolis**, known as ***Amun*** and coupled with ***Amaunet***. For others, he was a god of air, wind and atmosphere, who came from Middle Egypt. For others again, he was born in **Thebes**, which would explain why his main shrine was in this city. But, whatever ***Amun's*** origins, it seems perfectly clear that until the Middle Kingdom, his part in the religious organization of the country was relatively small. On the other hand, after the 12th Dynasty his cult became very popular and ***Amun*** quickly became the dominant figure of the Egyptian Pantheon. As his reputation increased, the clergy decided to create a theology in complete harmony with his new personality.

The Theban cosmogony combined elements from **Hermopolis**, **Heliopolis** and **Memphis**, to which were added new attributes. It was told that at the beginning of time the snake ***Kematef***, *"the one who has accomplished his time,"* emerged from ***Nun*** at exactly the emplacement of the town of **Thebes**. He started the process of creation and, when his time was up, he gave birth to ***Irta*** *"the one who made the earth,"* and retired into a long sleep. ***Irta*** then began the creation of the universe. He started by creating the earth and the eight primeval gods who went to **Hermopolis**, **Memphis** and **Heliopolis** to give birth to the sun, to ***Ptah*** and ***Atum***. Exhausted by this colossal work, they came back to **Thebes**, and, just as ***Kematef*** and ***Irta***, went to sleep for ever. In this cosmogony, the Theban clergy wanted to make ***Amun*** the **Ba** of ***Kematef***, which meant that ***Amun***, as god of creation, appeared in the shape of ***Kematef***.

He was also called "the Hidden one," which meant *"the one whose nature escapes one's comprehension"*. This is ***Amun***'s specific characteristic: the nature of the king of gods was incomprehensible. **Herodotus** gave an account of a legend about ***Amun*** and his son ***Khons***. *"**Hercules,** they say, very much wanted to see **Zeus,** who didn't want to show himself to him. In the end, because of the obstinacy of **Hercules**, the god gave in. He killed a ram, took its head off, held it in front of his own face and skinned the animal and clothed himself with it: under this disguise he appeared to **Hercules**."* The names of ***Zeus*** and ***Hercules*** should be translated as ***Amun*** and ***Khons,*** for according to **Herodotus**, *"**Amun** is the name the Egyptians give to **Zeus**."* Thus, ***Hercules,*** son of ***Zeus*** and **Alcmene**, was none other than ***Khons***, son of ***Amun*** and ***Mut***. In many cases, the different animal appearances assumed by a god are a kind of screen used to be unrecognizable, or to confuse another god. The image of the ram is the symbol of all creative forces, those of the sun as those that allow the reproduction of living beings. This subterfuge allows ***Amun*** to indirectly answer his son's question, without revealing his real nature. In this story, one must understand that ***Amun*** has gradually acquired a personality in close relation with the sun and fertility: under the aspect of ***Amun-Re'***, he has assumed the characteristics of the solar god of **Heliopolis**, and under the one of ***Amun-Min***, he has become a fecund god of creation.

The attributes as supreme god of the Kingdom gave him a special role in the kingdom. After the New Kingdom, the Pharaoh became the carnal son of ***Amun***: he was the result of a union between the god and the royal wife. This filiation created a bond between the world of gods and the world of men; and it explains the prestige of the royal function, founded on a pharaoh who was the embodiment of the supreme god and his representative on earth.

**Amun and Mut**

*This statuary group, known as the Ma'atmeri, presents the god of the Kingdom, Amun, accompanied by his wife the goddess Mut. Amun wears his crown composed of a mortar and two high stylized feathers. Small details show that Mut is the vulture goddess: she is wearing a dress with straps decorated with vulture wings, and on her head she carries a representation of the bird. She is wearing the pschent, the double royal crown of Upper and Lower Egypt, and on her forehead is a cobra, called the uraeus, which was supposed to overpower the enemies of the pharaoh. Both are seated on a throne decorated with alternating highly symbolic signs: the ankh, a cruciform insignia representing life; the was scepter representing the divine, and the djed pillar, a symbol of stability.*

New Kingdom.

## Anubis

Anubis 

*Illegitimate son of Osiris and Nephthys*

*He presides over the embalming rituals and is the intermediary between the deceased and the Judgment Hall; the official guardian of the necropolis*

*Principal place of worship: Cynopolis (Middle Egypt)*

*Representation: jackal or man with the head of a jackal*

The appearance of ***Anubis*** is determined by the part he plays in the Egyptian pantheon. Just as ***Wepwawet*** of **Asyut** and ***Khentimentiu*** of **Abydos**, he belongs to the group of canine divinities. He is depicted as a jackal, and recalls the dogs that haunted the desert surrounding the necropolis. By assimilation, certain funeral deities have been given the appearance of these animals and have become the keepers of the dwellings of eternity.

***Anubis*** is supposedly the illegitimate son of ***Osiris*** and ***Nephthys***. According to legend, after ***Osiris*** was murdered by his brother ***Seth***, ***Isis*** discovered that she had

been betrayed by her husband, who had had relations with her sister ***Nephthys***. A son was born of this union: ***Anubis***. A crown of sweet clover left by ***Osiris*** on ***Nephthy's*** bed gave ***Isis*** the definite proof of the god's infidelity. But it seems that ***Osiris*** had mistaken one sister for another... Afraid of the wrath of her official husband ***Seth***, ***Nephthys*** hid the baby in the marshes. ***Isis***, who unfortunately couldn't have a child with her husband went and searched for him. She travelled throughout the country and finally found him: she fed him and brought him up to be her warder and most faithful companion.

Chronologically in this myth, ***Anubis*** was born once ***Osiris*** has already died: one supposes that the mating had taken place just before the god was murdered; on the contrary, ***Anubis*** was begotten before ***Horus***, as ***Horus*** is ***Osiris***'s posthumous child. The tale of the "**Legend of Osiris**" says that after ***Seth*** had dismembered ***Osiris***'s body, ***Anubis*** helps ***Isis*** and ***Nephthys*** put the dead god's body back together again. Then ***Anubis*** participates in the rites designed to give life back to ***Osiris***'s body. He makes the first mummy, and thus becomes one of the main protagonists of ***Osiris***'s resurrection. This is when ***Horus*** appears. It is said that after ***Anubis*** has reconstituted ***Osiris***'s body, ***Isis*** magically conceives from her dead husband: she gives birth to little ***Horus***, the direct and legitimate successor of ***Osiris***.

It is therefore quite natural, considering his part in the resurrection of ***Osiris***, that ***Anubis*** shall become the god of the embalmers and the god responsible for the deceased in the afterworld. In most cases, when the defunct arrives at the gates of the Underworld, it is he who is the go-between. At the term of his journey, when the deceased presents himself before ***Osiris***, it's ***Anubis*** who is the intermediary between the newcomer and his judges: he ushers the deceased into the tribunal and proceeds to the weighing of the heart. Later, if the deceased for some reason or other wants to go back to earth, he must inform ***Anubis***; this last escape will be possible only with his agreement duly written down in the form of a decree.

Because of his multiple functions, ***Anubis*** has several titles, all in direct relation to his essential part in the survival of the deceased: he is *"the Lord of the Mummy Wrappings"* as the god of the embalmers, *"President of the Divine Pavilion"* which is the name of the building where the mummification ceremonies take place, *"Lord of the Necropolis"* or *"the One who is sitting on his Mountain"* as the guardian of the tombs and the guide to the deceased in the meanders of the lower world. We know quite a lot about ***Anubis*** thanks to the reliefs and texts that have been found in the royal and civil tombs in the Nile valley. One shouldn't forget, though, that during the pharaonic period, ***Anubis*** remained very popular in all the religious centers of the country, especially **Thebes** and **Memphis**. His main sanctuary is in Middle Egypt, in **Cynopolis**, the "City of the Dogs".

*Next pages*

**Anubis and the deceased**

*Many tombs present this scene in which Anubis, delicately bending over the deceased, prepares the mummy and proceeds to the rites necessary for a proper preservation of the body. This is his natural function, as he is the inventor of mummification, a technique he invented to save the god Osiris who had been murdered by Seth. Thus the rites that are conducted on all the deceased and on every mummy must reproduce, in the very smallest details, the ceremony by which Osiris was brought back to life.*

Tomb 1 of Sennedjem,
Deir el-Medina, New Kingdom,
West Thebes, Upper Egypt.

**Paser before Anubis and Hathor**

*You can see several kinds of scenes on the side of the coffins: cosmogonic scenes, scenes from the "Book of the Dead," scenes of personal piety or referring to the voyage of the deceased in the Underworld... The images often vary according to the period and personality of the owner: his social rank, his home town and his convictions are as many elements that can influence the iconography of the coffin. There is no rule, but of course the deceased will prefer "useful" pictures, that will ensure him a life among the blessed. Thus it is considered right to be represented next to divinities or funerary deities. Here, Paser, who was a priest of Amun in Thebes, has chosen to be represented in a scene where he offers incense to two deities he will have to reconcile in the Underworld: the jackal Anubis, god of the embalmers and the cow Hathor, protector of the Theban necropolis.*

Third Intermediary Period.

# *Apis*

*Apis* 

*Son of a cow made fertile by Ptah*

*Sacred bull representing Ptah on earth, equally associated with Osiris and Re'*

*Principal place of worship: Memphis (Lower Egypt)*

*Representation: a bull wearing the solar disc on its forehead*

*Sacred bulls were buried in the Serapeum in Memphis*

An Egyptian divinity can appear to its subjects under various guises. It usually appears under the aspect of the statue of the cult, in which it is said that the god resides. But frequently the god appears in the body of a specific animal: ***Horus*** as a falcon or hawk, ***Thoth*** as an ibis, ***Sobek*** as a crocodile, ***Bastet*** as a cat… Each animal becomes the visible manifestation of the divinity it represents. This is why living images of the cult were kept and honored in the temples: these are the famous "sacred animals" that travelers in Antiquity wrote about, all of them shocked at this particular cult that was present everywhere from north to south in the country. The cult of sacred animals appeared in the earliest period, but grew very popular in the Late Period. Within the walls of the temples, several thousand animals were entrusted to breeders, who were responsible for having a prosperous breed for the needs of the cult. The necropolis, which contained large amounts of mummified corpses of sacred animals, date back to this period.

The cult of bulls follows this logic. At the beginning, ***Apis*** symbolizes fecundity and is the representative animal of procreation. As time went by, he acquires many more qualities: he is associated with the king and other deities. He becomes the official representation and incarnation of ***Ptah***, the creative god of Memphis. Later, he acquired solar and funeral features borrowed from ***Re'*** and ***Osiris***. His cult then becomes very important in Egypt as he symbolizes, by himself, the three main facets of the divine nature: creation (***Ptah***), life (***Re'***), and death (***Osiris***). His main residence is in **Memphis**: ***Apis*** rules south of ***Ptah***'s temple.

The choice of a sacred animal depended on a certain number of criteria imposed by the clergy of the god he represented. Unlike certain cults where the sacred animal was changed every year, the bull ***Apis*** was an animal chosen for several distinctive signs, and it embodied the god until its death. *"The bull who is given the name of Apis has the following signs: it is black with a white triangle on his forehead, it has an eagle patch on its back, the hairs of its tail are split and it has a beetle sign under its tongue"* writes **Herodotus**. When an ***Apis*** bull died, ***Ptah***'s clergy began an urgent search all over the country to find a calf with these marks. After it had been found, it was brought to **Memphis**, where it stayed until the end of its days as the sacred animal. It had a harem of cows, as well as priests to look after it and take care of its comfort night and day. The bull ***Apis*** was believed to be born of a cow impregnated by ***Ptah*** who appeared as a celestial light.

Here again, **Herodotus** gives us this detail: *"This **Apis** is a bull born of a cow, which, from then on, can't bear any more calves. The Egyptians say that lightning comes down from heaven on the animal, which is thus made pregnant, and gives birth to the **Apis** bull."* The mother cow had the same privileges as its son: it had its own sacred space in ***Ptah***'s sanctuary, was given a sumptuous funeral, and was an object of cult during its life and after its death.

If one believes the narratives of the travelers of the time, the funeral of an ***Apis*** bull had to be spectacular, as it was very similar to the funeral of a human being. In the same way, the bull was embalmed: the body on one side, and the viscera on the other. The operation lasted seventy days, then the remains were brought to the valley temple, located close to the Nile, and then to the funeral temple, close to the necropolis. Most of the tombs of the sacred bulls are in **Saqqara**, in a place called the **Serapeum**. There are several underground galleries connected with sepulchral rooms, apt to receive the sarcophagi of the bulls. These chambers can still be seen and are amazing: they are generally made out of black granite and measure about 14 feet long, 7 feet wide and 10 feet high. Twenty four sarcophagi of this kind have been discovered in the underground of the **Serapeum**. In earlier periods, the bulls were buried in wooden coffins that disintegrated. But many objects found around the necropolis - figurines, statues or **ushabtis** - give us an idea of the importance of this cult from the beginning of the New Kingdom onwards.

**The Apis bull**

*The necropolis of the Apis bulls, usually called the Serapeum of Memphis, was discovered in 1851 by a French archaeologist, Auguste Mariette. It has several underground galleries that lead into big rooms where the sarcophagi of the sacred bulls were placed. The tombs were probably walled in after the funeral of the animals. But nothing prevented the faithful from entering the Serapeum and leaving an ex-voto there. There are hundreds of these testimonies of individual piety. They are generally stelae, of different qualities, that have been fitted in the walls close to the entrances of the tombs. Usually they represent a person, the donor of the stela worshipping Apis, who was considered to be the incarnation of Ptah on earth and associated with Re' and Osiris.*

Late Period.

# Apophis

| Apophis 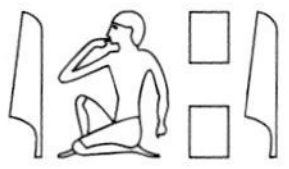 |
|---|
| Cosmic enemy and symbol of evil and all destructive forces |
| Representation: a giant snake |

Very few documents relate the apparition of the snake ***Apophis***. In fact, only the temple of **Esna** (Upper Egypt) contains a precise reference to the origin of this monster. The text explains that ***Apophis***, *"the one that was spat out,"* was born of goddess ***Neith's*** saliva which had fallen in the primeval waters: the former gods spurned the spittle, which caused ***Apophis*** to be perpetually in revolt. He symbolizes evil, all destructive forces and the power of chaos. He is the main enemy of the gods, the cosmic enemy, who every morning and every evening attacks the solar boat with the intention of overthrowing it, so as to stop the process of creation. This eternal fight, which represents the continuous assault of confusion on an organized world, is constantly alluded to in the documents about the voyages of the sun, especially in the "**Book of What is in the Tuat**", the **Tuat** being the Underworld.

***Apophis*** is depicted as a gigantic snake that lives in the depths of darkness. It is believed that beyond the created world, there is an abyss where one finds the sinners, the ones who haven't been saved at the judgment of the dead, and the enemies of the gods, namely the snake ***Apophis***. Darkness symbolized non-existence: those who are put there don't exist anymore. Every day, ***Apophis*** emerges from darkness to assault the sun god; every day he is defeated, and condemned to return to this non-existence. This symbol will be used afterwards in the Greco-Roman period with ***Uroboros***, *"the one who swallows his tail."* The image of the complete circle of the body of the snake illustrates the nothingness that surrounds the organized world everywhere.

**The fight against the snake Apophis**

*From the New Kingdom onwards, a funerary text, written on papyrus or on leather, accompanies the deceased into the other world. The "Book of the Dead," called "Formula to Make the Sun Rise" by the ancient Egyptians, has a hundred and ninety chapters that are supposed to ensure a happy existence to the deceased in the hereafter. It is a book of various incantations with illustrations; its presence and reading are supposed to resuscitate and deify, give freedom of movement and anything that was needed in the Underworld. Anything can be useful: one may need to eat, one may fear to die a second time, one may want to come back to earth, one might meet bad spirits, and, among others, one may have to face the snake Apophis, the monster of destruction who never ceases to be a peril for the world's balance. Whatever the situation, one must immediately know the formula to say in case of danger, or when one wants something in particular. That's what "Book of the Dead" is for: to offer the deceased the keys necessary for his protection, his survival and his happiness in the Underworld.*

New Kingdom.

Two deities take a more specific part in the destruction of ***Apophis:*** the goddess ***Isis*** and her brother, ***Seth***. ***Isis*** uses her talents as a magician to bewitch the snake. Standing just at the front of the solar boat, she conjures him and her magic touches the terrifying monster: he loses all his senses and is no longer able to locate himself. These handicaps make the annihilation of ***Apophis*** easier, especially as the gods have been given many eyes and ears in order to fight the snake ***Apophis***. As for ***Seth***, the god of evil and thunder, he was named by the solar god ***Re'*** himself to appear among the members of the solar boat where he is the main defender against the constant attacks of the monster of destruction.

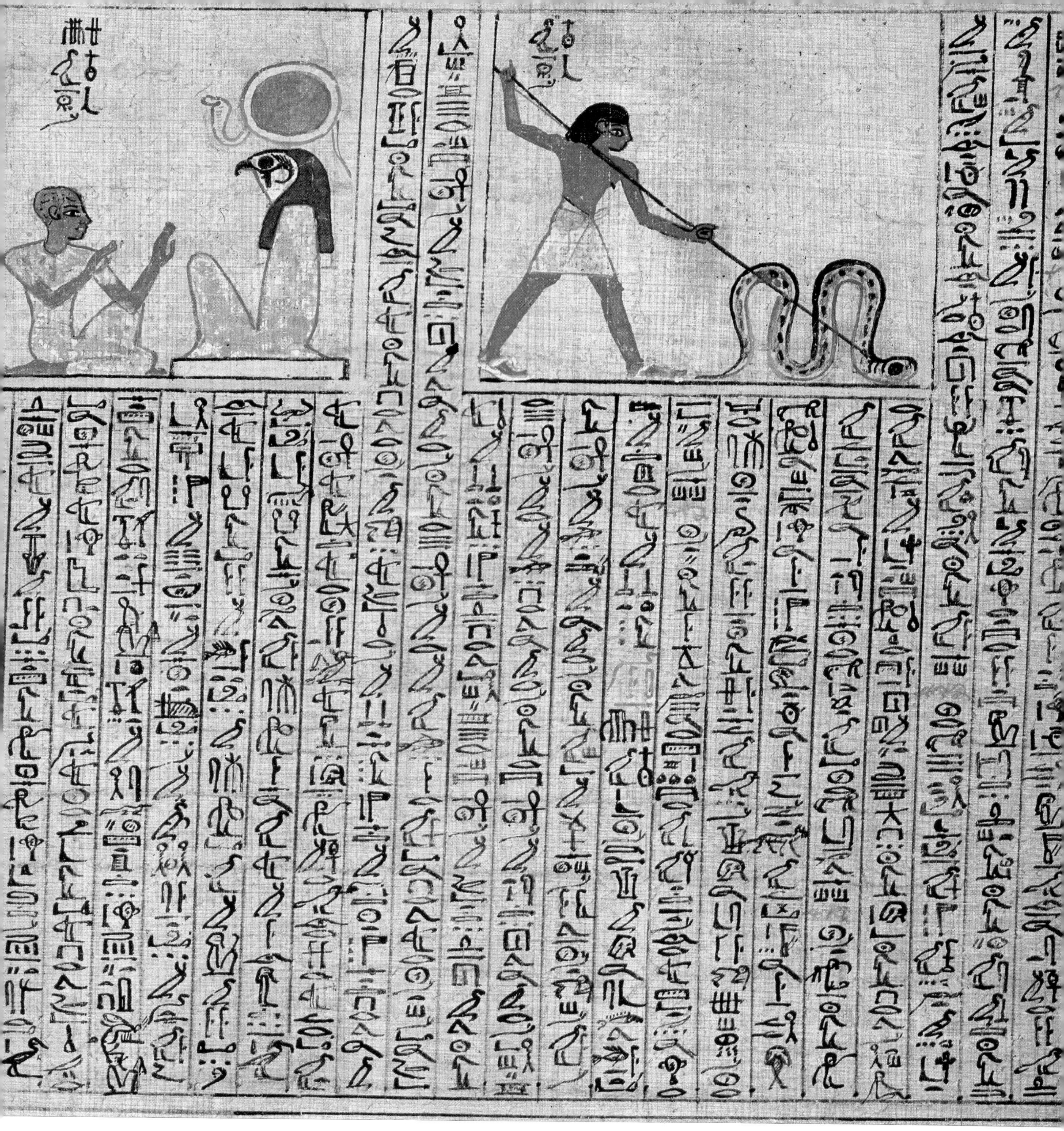

In the everyday life of the ancient Egyptians, this fight is illustrated by the numerous bewitching rites that are supposed to repel hostile forces in general, and ***Apophis*** in particular. Little figurines, on which was engraved the name of ***Apophis***, were made in one of the animal forms the malevolent snake was supposed to take (hippopotamus, tortoise or oryx). After the incantation had been pronounced, the figurine face was lacerated and it was thrown into the fire. In the same way, the deceased never forgot to protect himself against the eventual assaults of ***Apophis*** in the other world. The Chapter 39 of the "**Book of the Dead**", called *"How to repel the demon **Apophis**,"* is a long exorcism intended to keep the power of the evil snake away.

# *Aten*

Aten 

*Solar and creative god at the time of Amenhotep IV*

*Principal place of worship: Tell el-Amarna (Middle Egypt)*

*Representation: a solar disc, with long rays ended by hands holding crosses of life*

In the Egyptian pantheon, many deities incarnate the sun, and particularly its creative and vital force. All the gods which manifest the power of the sun assume a human or animal representation, and adopt specific attributes allowing men to recognize and honor them. This is true, for instance, for ***Harakhty*** ***"Horus*** of the Horizon," who is represented as a man with the head of a hawk upon which sits a solar disc. The same goes for the god of **Thebes**, ***Amun-Re'***, depicted as a man wearing a high crown with two feathers bordering a solar disc. But if you want to name the sun itself in its visible appearance, or the solar disc, you use the name of ***Aten***.

The name of ***Aten*** was mentioned first in the Old Kingdom, in the "**Pyramid Texts**", and it designated the sun. Not until the 18th Dynasty, and especially the reign of *Amenhotep III*, did his cult make a small apparition. But it is *Amenhotep IV*, better known under the name of *Akhenaten*, who elevated, for a while, the worship of ***Aten*** to its supreme height: that of a dynastic deity. Many speculations have been made to explain this religious upheaval. For some, it was for political reasons; others insist upon the religious foundation of the heresy; still others insist upon the peculiar personality of *Amenhotep IV*... In fact the truth probably lies in all three theses: a political context dominated by ***Amun***'s clergy; a desire to glorify the sun in its most obvious and glorious manifestation, the disc; and a strange personality: both a thinker and philosopher, as well as a fanatic and mystic.

The reign of *Amenhotep III* is marked by a consciousness of the tremendous power wielded by the clergy of ***Amun,*** the *"king of the gods."* It is so powerful that its lawful representative, the High Priest, is as important as any of the main dignitaries in the country: he has the head of immense divine properties and upon which the royal administration has no hold. It is only under the reign of *Akhenaten* that the measures taken to minimize his influence have any result: in the year IV, the king definitely cuts off from ***Amun***'s clergy, leaves the town of **Thebes,** and builds a new capital in **Akhetaten** "the Horizon of ***Aten***."

On a site *"disclosed by **Aten** himself,"* a city grows where the royal family and the court exclusively worship ***Aten,*** who, alone, becomes the universal and creative god; the *"father of the fathers and mother of the mothers."* Theoretically, this new cult put the perception of the divine within the grasp of any worshipper, since, to adore ***Aten*** one just needs to address the sun. But in fact the effective presence of the god in the sky does not necessarily mean that his comprehension is easy: the essence itself of ***Aten*** remains invisible to the common mortal. So he needs an intermediary in order to manifest himself, as there is no picture, statue or sacred animal to represent him on earth. And who better than *Akhenaten*, to play this part of mediator... Thus Pharaoh becomes the only prophet of the god, and the representative of ***Aten*** to his subjects. The faithful prays at home, in front of an altar upon which is a representation of the king. The artistic style that develops during this whole heretical period reminds one of the fundamental part played by *Akhenaten*. He embodies the creative god, who, whatever the beliefs, is an androgynous deity because calling to mind the asexual unity preceding creation. He is therefore represented with attributes of both sexes: a man with a strange long face, swollen belly, wide hips and almost feminine breasts.

This role as an intermediary appears also on the reliefs of tombs and the cult stelae. Usually, according to tradition, the deceased is represented on the sides of his grave with the deities of the next world, those who will be able to open the doors of the afterworld for him. Here, ***Aten***, because of his qualities as universal god, also takes care of the dead, usurping the prerogatives of ***Osiris***. On earth as in the other world, the presence of an official mediator is essential. This is why, in the funerary representations, the main role in the scene is played by *Akhenaten*, pushing the owner of the tomb into the background. The scenes present the Pharaoh worshipping the sun, which shines with rays ended by hands. The shafts of light carry the **ankh** cross, symbol of life, that the king breathes in; through this simple act, ***Aten*** becomes the god dispenser of life, the one upon whom all existence lies.

**The solar disc Aten**

*The site of Tell el-Armana, capital of the Kingdom under the reign of Amenhotep IV-Akhenaten, encloses some civilian tombs dug into the Arabian cliff. The reliefs that can be seen on the walls of different hypogea are of very unequal quality, especially as most have been badly treated by the worshippers of Amun. To erase the memory of the Amarnian heresy, the face and name of those who elevated Aten to the highest rank in the Egyptian pantheon have been systematically knocked off. For this reason the tombs are generally undecipherable as so many people and texts have been mutilated. This scene shows the main actors of the Amarnian cult: Aten darting his rays extended by hands towards the royal family, Akhenaten and Nefertiti worshipping the disc and the little royal princesses waving a sistrum in front of the deity. All the subjects show the iconographical characteristics of the Amarnian period: long faces, prominent skulls, thin busts, wide hips and thighs.*

Civilian tomb, New Kingdom,
Tell el-Amarna,
Middle Egypt.

### The Heliopolitan Ennead

*The Ennead of Heliopolis is an association of nine gods who are the incarnation of the elementary powers of the organized world. This Ennead, imagined by the theologians of the holy town of Heliopolis, has three generations of deities that came from the creative god, the sun god: Re'-Atum-Khepri: Shu and Tefenet; Geb and Nut; Osiris, Isis, Horus the Elder, Seth and Nephthys.*

## *Atum*

Atum 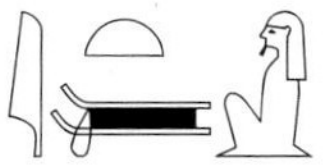

Creative god of Heliopolis, incarnating the setting sun
Principal place of worship: Heliopolis (Lower Egypt)
Representation: man (without any specific attribute)

***Atum*** is one of the basic principles of the Egyptian theology. He is a solar and creative god, mainly worshipped in **Heliopolis**. To understand their real nature, one must know that each deity of the pantheon is endowed with "**kheperu**". This word has no translation: it designates the many short-lived and complementary personalities a god may adopt. Each one of these particularities is only a facet of the god's personality, that for a time, he is totally invested in. For instance, the different phases of the sun's journey through the sky are considered to be "**kheperu**" of the sun and have the following names: ***Khepri***, the rising sun, ***Re'***, the sun in all its splendor, and ***Atum***, the setting sun. All three incarnate the sun, but each one only represents one aspect of the solar entity. Very often, the myths and legends call this creative god of the cosmogony of **Heliopolis**, the "Universal Master." One should understand that he is the sun, but if he must be named, one can use indifferently the names of ***Khepri***, ***Atum***, ***Re'***, ***Re'-Atum-Khepri***, ***Re'-Atum***...

***Atum***'s role begins in **Heliopolis**, "the City of the Sun." Here the theologians drew up a cosmogony that presented a creative god and nine primeval gods: the great Ennead of Heliopolis. The texts explain that before the creation was ***Nun***, chaos and nothingness. Out of this watery chaos, an unconscious force slowly emerged and

## The Great Ennead of Heliopolis

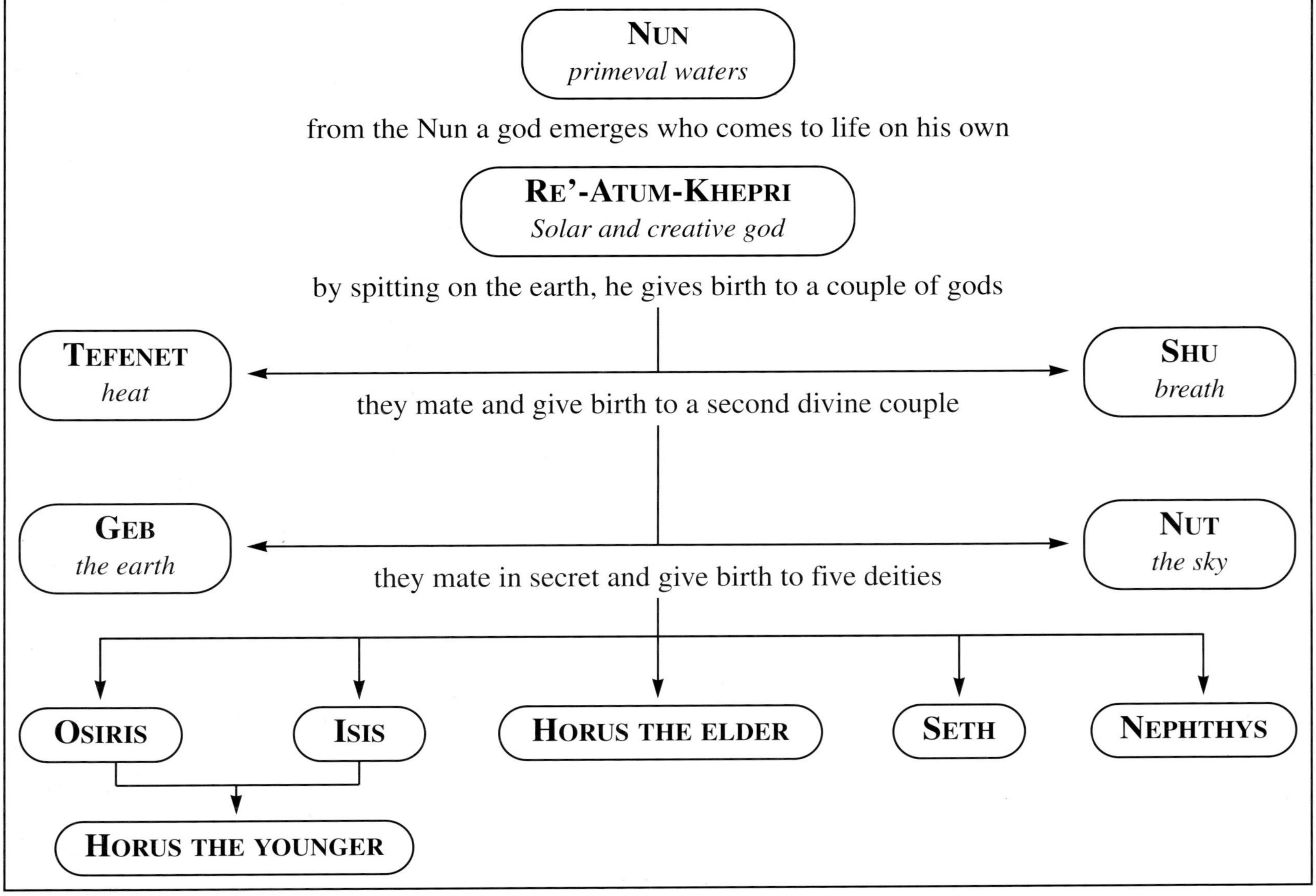
Nun
primeval waters
from the Nun a god emerges who comes to life on his own
Re'-Atum-Khepri
Solar and creative god
by spitting on the earth, he gives birth to a couple of gods
Tefenet
heat
Shu
breath
they mate and give birth to a second divine couple
Geb
the earth
Nut
the sky
they mate in secret and give birth to five deities
Osiris
Isis
Horus the Elder
Seth
Nephthys
Horus the Younger

was born to life by dissociating itself from ***Nun***, thus becoming a whole being. He has neither father nor mother, and is his own creator, since he is the *"one that is born to life from himself"*: generally the Egyptians used the name of ***Atum*** to qualify this first being. One understands therefore why this demiurge has several personalities. A few lines from the "**Book of the Dead**" explain this apparent ambiguity: *"I am **Atum** when I manifest myself in the **Nun**; but I am **Re'** in his brilliant appearance, when he is ready to govern what he has created."* So ***Atum*** is to be understood as a principle representing a potentiality of creation, and ***Re'*** as the motor incarnating the realization of this creation. Being conscious of the fact that he is living, the demiurge began his creation by making himself a physical body. It is said that he appeared under this form in **Heliopolis** on a pyramidal stone, the **benben**, which evokes a sun ray turning into stone. Now, ***Atum*** can start the creation: *"then my spirit showed its efficiency, the project of creation appeared in front of me, and as I was alone, I did what I wanted to do."* The **Bremmer-Rhind papyrus** shows how much the creation shall be considered as a willful act of the demiurge. Nevertheless, the intellectual aspect of the creation cannot be dissociated from the physiological act that brought beings and objects into existence. And the texts never fail to give all the details. Another excerpt of the same document explains how ***Atum*** gave birth to ***Shu*** and ***Tefenet***, the first divine couple: *"I united myself to my own body, so that they came out of me, after I had produced the excitement with my hand, that my desire had been satisfied with my hand and that the semen had fallen from my mouth."* The first couple is born thanks to the will and the action of the demiurge. Afterwards, many generations of gods will come to existence according to the natural procedure.

## Re'-Atum-Khepri

*In the cosmogony of Heliopolis, the creation of the world is attributed to the solar god. This deity appears under a triple identity called Re'-Atum- Khepri. In the morning, he is Khepri, the rising sun; he has the appearance of a scarab. At noon, he is Re', the sun at its zenith; he is represented by a solar disc. In the evening, he is Atum, the setting sun; he has the aspect of a man with the head of a ram or of an old man. This image comes from the tomb of Sethos II and illustrates the particularity of the solar god: the beetle of Khepri, the solar disc Re' and the man of Atum appear in a beautifully carved representation.*

Tomb 15 of Sethos II, Valley of the Kings, New Kingdom, West Thebes, Upper Egypt.

# Bastet

Bastet 

*Daughter of the sun and eye of the star, she incarnates the peaceful features of dangerous deities, such as the lioness Sakhmet*

*Principal place of worship: Bubastis (Lower Egypt)*

*Representation: a cat or a woman with a cat's head*

Several Egyptian goddesses are supposed to be the daughters of ***Re'***, the sun: ***Hathor***, ***Tefenet***, ***Sakhmet***, ***Maat***, ***Bastet***... Whatever their name, they appear as the eye of the sun. Each one symbolizes a part of the radiance of the sun and adopts, according to the needs of this function, appearances and names that vary according to the myths in which they are integrated. As incarnations of solar radiance, they become the necessary implements for the permanence and stability of the creation, as it is only the projection of this vital energy that allows the solar god to guarantee the continuity of existence.

Their mission in the cosmic organization is double and conflicting: they have to stay close to the sun, but constantly move away from it at the same time. They cannot leave their father because they have to feed him and regenerate every day. A few lines from the "**Coffin Texts**" describe this essential function. We are at the beginning of the creation, just after the solar god has begotten the first divine couple: *"Breathe in your daughter **Ma'at**, bring her up to your nose to make your heart live. That your daughter **Ma'at** and your son **Shu**, whose name is also Life, don't leave you."*

The daughters of the sun must also spread the light on earth; they are therefore often called upon to leave their father and go to the farthest places on earth, for the unique purpose of pushing the darkness as far away as possible. Myths were created to solve this ambivalence; they explain and justify the constant comings and goings of the daughters of the sun. Like their missions, their personalities are ambiguous. They very often have two totally contradictory facets: they are at the same time destructive and beneficent, formidable and peaceful. Their aggressive aspect is due to their permanent fight against the forces and powers of chaos; their peaceful aspect suggests their fundamental part in the permanence of creation.

There is a goddess, daughter of the sun, whose name is ***Bastet***: she embodies the pacific features of the dangerous goddesses, particularly of the lioness ***Sakhmet***. It seems that the Egyptians found it difficult to dissociate these two deities, to such an extent that they talked of them as being one only person: calm and lovable under the name of ***Bastet***, formidable and destructive under the aspect of ***Sakhmet***. In her primitive form, she was represented as a woman with the head of a lioness, holding the **ankh** cross, symbol of life, in one hand, and a scepter in the other. Later her iconography becomes the cat. Either she is a cat, majestically sitting up and covered with jewels, or she is a woman with a cat's head, holding a musical instrument or a sistrum; then again she can be represented as a mother cat feeding her kittens. This last representation often gave her the role in Egyptian households as patroness of maternity.

Her main place of worship is in the Delta, in the actual **Tell Basta**. In those days, the town was called **Per-Bastet**, the "House of ***Bastet***," a name that the Greeks turned into **Bubastis**. It is **Herodotus** who gives us one of the best descriptions of the site that today is in ruins, but according to him, must have been superb: *"In this town, there is a temple dedicated to the goddess **Bastet** that must be mentioned: others may be more imposing or rich, but no other gives the eyes so much pleasure."* He talks about a sanctuary in the middle of the town surrounded by two large canals that give the site the aspect of an island. Inside, he says *"a wood planted with tremendous trees surrounds a vast shrine in which sits the statue of the goddess."* He adds that a road leaves the temple and leads to a chapel dedicated to ***Thoth***, and is *"bordered with trees that reach the sky."* In another chapter, **Herodotus**, visibly fascinated by the cult of this goddess, explains about the religious ceremonies: *"The main and most popular festivity takes place in Bubastis, in the honor of **Artemis** (**Bastet**)... When the Egyptians go to the Bubastis festivities, this is what they do: they go on the river, a great many men and women, a big crowd on each boat... When they arrive in Bubastis, they worship the goddess with big sacrifices and drink more grape wine during this festivity than during the whole rest of the year. According to local people, there are some seven hundred thousand visitors that go there, men and women together (not counting the children)."*

**The goddess Bastet**

*Bastet, the cat goddess, embodies the peaceful and conciliating features of the dangerous and terrifying goddesses. This is probably why her cult is so popular all along the Nile Valley. She is beneficent, peaceful, lovable and calm. Her name evokes sweetness, peace and rest. Women consider her to be a protector of households and births. She appears under different iconographies, according to which aspect the artist wanted to emphasize: a mother cat feeding her kittens, a cat sitting up or a woman with a cat's head. The hundreds of statuettes, mummies or cat amulets made in her honor, and found in sanctuaries prove that she was a particularly popular goddess with the Egyptians.*

Late Period.

# Bes

Bes 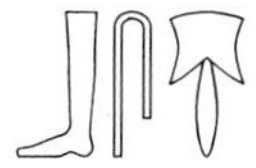

*A familiar god, patron of homes, pregnant women and children*

*Principal place of worship: at home, and during the Greek period in the temple of Sethos I in Abydos*

*Representation: a bearded dwarf, with bow legs and an amiable face, frontally represented*

There are dozens of small gods that coexist alongside the great deities of the Egyptian pantheon, and their role is to protect men in their everyday life. They certainly have not the abilities of the great gods of the cosmogony, but that isn't the point: they were created by the people and for the people who gave them a caricaural appearance.

***Bes*** belongs to this category of gods, very helpful in adversity and very popular in Egyptian homes. Just his appearance is meant to give joy and good temper. He's a bearded and misshapen dwarf, with crooked legs and a cheerful face. ***Bes*** is always frontally represented, which is unusual in Egyptian stylistic traditions, showing people through their profile. His main role is to protect men against evil beings or bad influences, reptiles, scorpions or other dangerous animals, and generally against all evil spirits. He drives malevolent spirits and the evil eye away with his grotesque dances and horrible grimaces. In the villages he watches over women in childbirth and their babies, and he looks after their homes. By night, when everything is so quiet, he is believed to protect the sleep of those who are resting peacefully by driving the hostile powers away.

Thus his presence is essential: it is strongly recommended to permanently wear an amulet with his effigy. Also, at home a small altar dedicated to the domestic cult is found in the main room. Little earthenware and terracotta figurines of the popular god ***Bes*** are put there, alongside other objects that had numerous virtues. Amongst these are stelae called "**Horus on the crocodiles**": ***Horus,*** depicted as a naked young man shown frontally, holds tightly reptiles or wild animals while trampling on crocodiles. His head is surmounted with an image of the god ***Bes***. A few lines of incantations and magic texts are engraved on the back: *"You protect me against all the wild beasts of the desert, all the crocodiles of the river, all the snakes and scorpions, all the insects that bite with their mandibles and sting with their tail, all the kinds of reptiles that attack in their caves."* The traditional explanation is that, to protect oneself against all these misfortunes, attacks or stings of poisonous animals or wild beasts, one just needs to sprinkle the stela with water and drink while saying these magical words.

For centuries, ***Bes*** acquired an unquestionable popularity, which allowed him to appear among the greatest gods of the Egyptian pantheon. Fabulous and mythical beings appear on the magical stelae of the Late Period, which are supposed to repel malevolent animals. These hybrid beings derive from several gods: ***Bastet***, ***Isis***, ***Horus*** and ***Bes***. The young god ***Horus*** is also given the terrifying animal head of Bes, so as to increase the miraculous and healing virtues of certain propitiatory objects.

As far back as the beginning of the Greek Period, there is a great increase in the number of images of the god ***Bes***: he appears on a large number of reliefs and architectural elements in many sanctuaries in the Nile valley (**Dendara** or **Abydos**, for example) and on many amulets, figurines or statuettes. He even overshadows "***Horus*** the Child," the little ***Harpokrates***, who was also very popular.

In the funerary temple of *Sethos I* in **Abydos**, he had his own sacred space from where he gave oracles. His goodness convinced people to rest inside his sanctuary, and to have their dreams interpreted there. This oracle is said to have worked until the 4th century A.D. The requests, inscribed on papyrus or parchments are very revealing about the daily concerns of the people who lived in the Nile valley: all the questions regarding their future, their professional or family problems, their prospects of travel, their health, were precisely written down. The worshippers asked whether they will be sick or well, whether they will find a bride or whether they will be able to get rid of their wife, whether they will get a raise or be let go, whether their chief will get mad at them or whether he will look at their account books. In fact, the requests only deal with very material problems; people who consult the oracles seem to be much more preoccupied by daily concerns than by existential questions.

**The dwarf Bes**

*This is Bes, a chubby bearded dwarf with crooked legs and a beastly head, patron of women and children. His main role is to preserve happiness and peace in every home. With his grotesque dances and horrible grimaces, he drives malevolent spirits away, protects men against evil spirits and preserves the rest of the sleeper. This is why he is a particularly popular god for the commoners. During the Greek period, Bes becomes a member of the Egyptian pantheon with the great gods. His worship, which until then had mostly been a private affair, then enters the sanctuaries of the Nile valley; evidence of this is given in a relief that was found in the temple of the goddess Hathor in Dendara.*

Temple of Hathor,
Ptolemaic Period,
Dendara, Upper Egypt.

## Geb

Geb 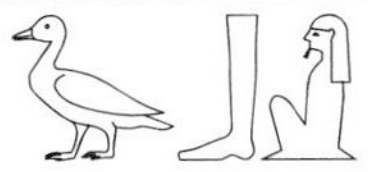

*Son of Shu, breath of life, and Tefenet, heat*

*Brother and husband of Nut, the goddess of the sky*

*Father of Osiris, Horus the Elder, Isis, Seth, and Nephthys*

*God personifying the earth*

*Representation: a man lying on the ground*

In the Heliopolitan creed, ***Geb*** and his sister and wife, the goddess ***Nut***, are a couple. Both were born of the union between ***Shu*** and ***Tefenet***, deities directly issued from the demiurge, the sun. ***Geb*** personifies the earth, whereas ***Nut*** symbolizes the sky. The legend explains that they were separated by the will of the creator. Seeing that ***Geb*** and ***Nut*** mated in secret, ***Re'*** ordered his son ***Shu*** to interfere. So ***Shu*** placed himself between the two, leaving ***Geb*** on earth and sending ***Nut*** into the sky. Thus ***Shu*** became the celestial space that separates the canopy of heaven from earth. Apart from the god ***Geb***, there are several other personifications of the earth: ***Pega***, ***Tanen***, ***Aker***… In fact, ***Geb*** symbolizes all the riches that are contained in the earth. The animals and minerals are under his control; hills, valleys and mountains are attributed to him.

***Geb*** is distinguished by his role amongst the royalty on earth. When the gods still reigned on earth, he sat on the throne of Egypt, just as his father ***Shu*** and his grandfather ***Atum*** had before him. A very interesting document, called "**the Royal Turin Canon**," contains the names and ruling

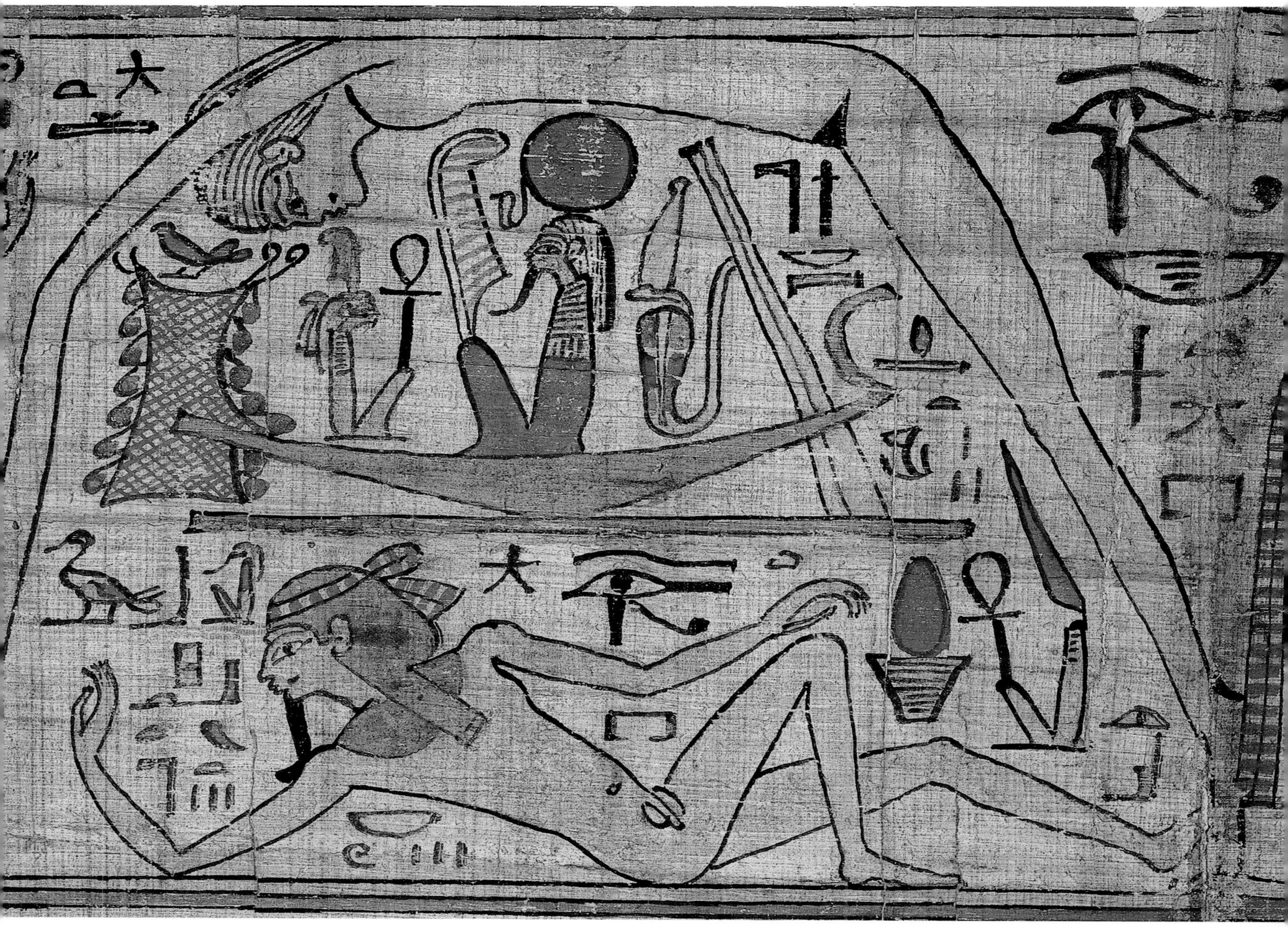

dates of these "god kings," most of whom belonged to the Heliopolitan family. In human royalties, the son becomes king at his father's death. In divine royalties, this rule of succession cannot apply because gods are immortal. One can simply establish, that for reasons we sometimes cannot fathom, the reigning god decides to withdraw in order to leave the throne to his son. As for the laws of succession, they seem to be identical to those defined for human royalties. A god may succeed his father, but his power will only be effective once he has received from the hands of ***Thoth***, the divine registrar, the record recognizing his legitimacy. Then his authority is extended to the created world: gods, human beings and elements.

When this narrative begins, men have already been created and they cohabit with the gods on earth. At the very beginning it is ***Atum***, the solar and creative god, who occupies the royal function. From his residence in **Heliopolis**, he watches over the proper unfolding of creation; apparently nothing seems to be able to disturb this peaceful reign. But as the years and centuries went by, the demiurge aged. And one day everyone, men and gods alike, decide to foment a rebellion that makes the sun god leave for the celestial heights. In a very logical manner, ***Shu*** succeeds his father. His first years of reign seem to have been peaceful: he is said to have built sanctuaries and towns, to watch over the steadiness of the world, and to protect with attention the boundaries of the universe so as to prevent the manifestation of cosmic enemies. Despite all these precautions, he is not able to avoid a rebellion, and after a fight against the forces of chaos, he leaves the earth with his attendants.

**Geb and Nut**

*The tale of creation in Heliopolis says that the sun emerged from chaos, and conceives Shu and Tefenet, who themselves give birth to Geb and Nut. These two gods secretly mate, but Re' disapproved of the union and asks his son to separate them. Shu sends Nut into the celestial heights, leaving Geb on earth. This extract from the Neskapashuty papyrus illustrates it. At the top, Nut represents the sky. At the bottom, Geb evokes the earth. Between the two bodies, Shu and Tefenet sit in a boat: they have just separated Nut, the sky from Geb, the earth.*

Third Intermediate Period.

While the divine assembly waits for ***Geb***'s legitimacy to be pronounced, it declares that his mother, ***Tefenet***, is to take over the regency. But, impatient, ***Geb*** rapes his mother just to prove that he is capable of ruling. He also learns that his predecessors had an invincible weapon: the uraeus, the sacred cobra with its hood extended, symbol of the solar eye. Placed on the sovereign's head, its virtue is to destroy the enemies of the sun. ***Geb*** then decides to get this weapon, even if he has to steal it from his father. With the help of a few followers, he tries to lay his hands on the divine cobra, which immediately reacts and burns the god's face. The future king, embarrassed, turns to the solar god to ask him for assistance. ***Re'*** then lent him his magic wig that immediately soothes his wound. If one really thinks about this story, it seems that ***Geb*** probably was the origin of the troubles that arose at the end of his father's reign.

Whatever the truth is, ***Geb*** sits on the throne of Egypt, and as the years go by, his reign acquires such prestige that the pharaohs are considered as the "sons of ***Geb***." The end of his reign is rather obscure. Some legends suggest there was a revolt against him led by ***Osiris***. To calm the rebels, ***Geb*** decides to kill his son. But quickly, he realizes what he has done, he brings ***Osiris*** back to life. Ashamed of himself, he leaves the earth and hands over the throne to his son.

# *Ha'py*

Ha'py

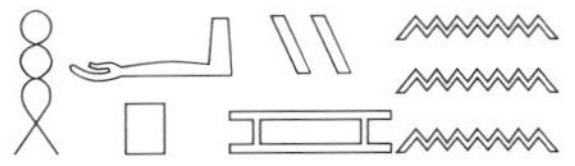

Personification of the Nile river, symbolizing inundation, fertility and abundance

Places of worship: he was adored all along the Nile river

Representation: an androgynous spirit with hanging breasts and swollen belly

Most elements of the cosmos and nature in the Egyptian religious system are represented by particular deities, totally different from the deities of the pantheon, called "personifications." They can designate natural principles or abstractions, places or localities, but most of them correspond to an economic reality, and evoke opulence and fertility. But no figure in the pantheon symbolizes the Nile as a river.

There are only some deities that, as figures of fecundity, incarnate abundance and inundation. These concepts are intimately linked to the Nile, but do not designate it as an element of the universe. Among these many personifications, the only one that really had his own existence and exceptional popularity, is ***Ha'py***, god of the floods.

In the texts, the Nile is considered to be a resurgence of the ***Nun***, the primeval ocean banished to the edges of the world by the creation. The sources of the earthly river are thought to be found in the ***Nun***. The god ***Ha'py*** represents the streams of the Nile: he gives strength to the floodwaters. He is therefore intimately bound to the ***Nun***, and must be considered as an entity fully participating from his nature. As the one responsible for the floods, ***Ha'py*** incarnates abundance and fertility. He is depicted as an androgynous figure with hanging breasts and swollen belly, holding the products of the Nile: flowers, fruits, fish... He is responsible for the fertility of the earth, and as such, protects all life. This is why his cult is very popular, and many offerings are made to him to pray for a sufficient flood for the country. Processions of alternatively feminine and masculine personifications of the Nile, are very often represented gracing the substructures of temples.

The Egyptians believe that the floods come from an underground cave close to the first cataract, and that there the god ***Khnum*** and the two goddesses ***Satis*** and ***Anukis*** who are associated with him, are the masters and guardians of the sources of the Nile. Their main function is to set free the right amount of silt needed to fertilize the cultivated fields of Egypt every year. It is ***Ha'py***, the guardian spirit of floods, who constitutes these reserves, and that is why the flood is often called "the arrival of ***Ha'py***." And that is also why it was advisable to throw food, sacrificed animals, amulets or feminine figurines in special places along the Nile to maintain its strength and healthy flooding. This extraordinary cult to the river spirit is logical enough if we remember that, all through Egyptian history, the flooding has been quite irregular: from the date of beginning to its volume and duration. In fact, more than half of the inundations are considered to be insufficient, which makes prayers to ***Ha'py*** essential to receive his benevolence.

**Ha'py, the Nile spirit**

*This androgynous being with hanging breasts, a swollen belly and a pleasant face is Ha'py: he is the manifestation of the flooding of the Nile. In a wider sense, he symbolizes fecundity and abundance. He ensures to Egypt the fertility of its fields, since flood and inundations, which bring the silt that serves as fertilizer, are under his control. He therefore is a very popular deity from the first cataract of the Nile to the Delta. Many offerings are brought to him and many statuettes are dedicated to him, in order to pray for the river to rise. This bronze work represents Ha'py kneeling and holding in his arms a table upon which are put the products of the Nile. His crown is divided in two: the little prop decorated with zigzags represents the water, or more precisely, the Nile; the three lotus buds, triumphantly emerging from the blessed river, represent the fertility of fields inundated by the flood.*

Late Period.

## The Sphinx Harmakhis

*A few hundred meters from the pyramid of King Khephren, sits Harmakhis "Horus on the Horizon," majestic guardian of the Giza necropolis. From the New Kingdom onwards, he acquires solar qualities which identify him with Re'-Atum-Khepri, the creative god of the cosmosgony of Heliopolis. Later, he assimilates the personality of Hurun, a foreign god brought in by a captive colony from Canaan. Both gods end by merging into an entity with solar characteristics, under the name of Hurun-Harmakhis. This recumbent lion is 65 feet high and 225 feet long. He was sculpted out of rock, probably under the reign of Khephren, to watch over the western funerary regions. He wears the royal traditional headdress, the nemes, and on its forehead, the uraeus, a cobra with its hood extended, which represents the eye of Re'.*

Sphinx of Khephren,
Old Kingdom,
Giza, Lower Egypt.

# *Harmakhis*

Harmakhis 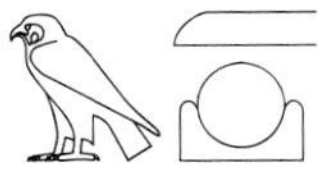

*"Horus on the Horizon"; in the 18th Dynasty, assimilation to Hurun, under the name of Hurun-Harmakhis*

*Solar god incarnated by the sphinx of Giza*

*Principal place of worship: Giza (Lower Egypt)*

*Representation: a sphinx with a human head*

Between the two paws of the great sphinx in **Giza** is a stela commemorating a dream *Tuthmosis IV* had, justifying his accession to the throne of Egypt. The history tells us how one day the young prince *Tuthmosis* stopped to rest in the shade of the great sphinx of **Giza**, after a long day of hunting in the desert. Tired, he fell deeply asleep. The god ***Harmakhis*** appeared to him in his dream and said to him:

*"Look at me and admire me, O my son Tuthmosis; it is I, your father **Harmakhis-Khepri-Re'-Atum**. I shall set you above men in royalty; you shall wear the white crown and the red crown on the throne of **Geb**, heir of gods. The country shall belong to you in all its length and all its width, as will everything that the Universal Master's bright eye shines upon. The food that comes from the Two Lands shall be for you; for you too, the impressive tributes of each foreign country; you shall also have a very long life. To you I turn my face and my heart; you are my protector and my guide. But, look, I am in the state of a man who suffers, for the sand of the desert upon which I crouch moves closer every day. So come nearer to me, that you may accomplish what I desire."*

So *Tuthmosis* had the sphinx cleared of the sand, and in exchange, ***Harmakhis*** gave him the throne. Of course this must be understood as a text of propaganda for *Tuthmosis IV*, as it seems that he wasn't the eldest son of *Amenhotep II* and Queen *Tiaa*. So his legitimacy must have been a little doubtful and he chose this premonitory dream to counter any opposition: he was chosen by the god ***Harmakhis*** himself to sit upon the throne of Egypt. From this day on, a specific cult grows around the sphinx of **Giza**. It becomes ***Harmakhis***, "***Horus*** on the Horizon," and assumes very pronounced solar features which linked him to the creative god ***Re'-Atum-Khepri***.

***Harmakhis*** lies to the east of the royal necropolis, at the beginning of the road that leads to the pyramid of *Khephren.* It is an enormous lion measuring 65 feet high and 225 feet long, initially carved to watch over the western regions, into which the sun and the deceased disappear. In the 18th and 19th Dynasties, when he takes on the functions of a solar god, ***Harmakhis*** is very popular.

His temple is enlarged, and brick walls built by *Tuthmosis IV* are added around it, into which hundreds of stelae are incorporated. With time, little chapels are built around the original sanctuary, and the sphinx of **Giza** rapidly becomes a popular pilgrimage destination. The pharaohs themselves honour him, and a tradition born directly from *Tuthmosis*'s dream was established: every new king had the sphinx cleared of sand. This might appear very symbolic, but during the Roman period, even the emperor *Nero* had the sphinx cleared of sand when he ascended the throne.

# *Haroeris*

Haroeris 

"Horus the Great" or "Horus the Elder"

Son of Geb, the Earth and Nut, the sky

Brother of Osiris, Isis, Seth and Nephtys

Principal place of worship: Kom Ombo (Upper Egypt)

Representation: a man with the head of a falcon

***Haroeris*** is "***Horus*** the Great" or "***Horus*** the Elder," god with the head of a falcon, particularly venerated in **Kom Ombo**, where he shares a sanctuary with ***Sobek,*** the crocodile god. There, he is associated in a triad with a goddess, ***Tasenetnofret***, the "Good Sister," and with a god-son, ***Panebtawi***, the "Master of the Two Countries." Some myths include him directly in the heliopolitan cosmogony: he would be one of the five children of the goddess ***Nut***, along with ***Osiris, Isis, Seth*** and ***Nephthys***. In this tradition, ***Horus the Elder***, the reigning god king, is in conflict with ***Seth.*** As usual the object of the dispute is the power of royalty ***Seth*** wants to seize. A duel is engaged between the two foes: as a result, ***Horus the Elder*** loses an eye and ***Seth*** his testicles. And each one leaves the scene of the fight with the humble trophy he keeps jealously.

We know that Egyptian religion is separated in two major trends, both very distinct but compatible. The first one tries to have a "scholarly" approach to the divine: elaborated by the priests, it defines the myths, legends and official faith. The second satisfies a popular request: its deities are closer to daily concerns. This private religion favors characters connected to the home, maternity and childhood, incarnated by ***Bes***, ***Isis*** and ***Harpokrates***. That is why so many figurines bearing their effigy have been found in settlements around houses or sometimes close to cemeteries, but never in temples.

This tends to show how much this production is secular, and exclusively reserved to homes: there were probably some rooms in the house with a little altar upon which an icon was set, and in front of which prayers were made. These statuettes and figurines are rather coarsely made and mostly in cast earthenware. The ones representing the little ***Harpokrates*** show him in all kinds of childish attitudes: the child plays, steals food, puts his hand in a pot of jam, goes for a walk, gets into a small boat or laughs carelessly. He often has the company of different animals (dogs or any kind of bird) and carries a cornucopia as a symbol: these two points establish his relationship with human fertility.

Sometimes the official tradition influences private beliefs. Then surprising images appear, in which popular deities become part of great cosmogonic myths. This is the case of a widely-found figurine from the Greco-Roman period, representing ***Harpokrates*** on a lotus flower. It is a reference to the tales of **Hermopolis**, that recall the beginning of the world: it is told that the demiurge, the true solar being, appeared in a lotus flower that emerged from the primeval waters. But we are nevertheless far from the official representations. The creative god is ***Harpokrates***, a plump boy comfortably seated on an outspread lotus bud. He holds a pot of food or a cornucopia, since he is at the source of all life, and he is wearing a radiating crown as a sign of his solar character. Other statuettes show him mounted on a ram or followed by a goose, animals that are traditionally attributed to ***Amun***, the supreme god of Egyptian Kingdom. And some figurines are ithyphallical; in this instance ***Harpokrates*** takes the place of the god of fertility, ***Min***.

# *Hathor*

Hathor 

*Daughter of Re', considered to be the eye of the sun*

*Wife of Horus (sometimes mother of Horus)*

*Goddess with several functions: celestial deity, Lady of Far Lands, Goddess of joy, Mistress of the Theban necropolis, Lady of the sycamore...*

*Principal place of worship: Dendara (Upper Egypt)*

*Representation: a woman with two horns surrounding the solar disc, a cow or a woman with a cow's head*

***Hathor***'s origins go back to the earliest times in Egypt's history, as her name appears in the oldest historical document known to this day, the "**Palette of Narmer**," a votive palette made out of schist, that recalls the unification of the two kingdoms of Egypt by *Narmer*, first pharaoh of the first dynasty. For the country, this event marks the passage from prehistoric times to history and inaugurates the pharaonic era. On the top part of the palette, both sides are adorned with heads of cows that symbolize the goddess ***Hathor***. What is the justification of her presence on this document? The palette was found in **Hierakonpolis**, the antique city of **Nekhen**, of which the patron god was ***Horus***. He appears here under a particular form: "***Horus*** the Younger," son of ***Hathor***, which makes the predominant location for his mother on the palette more understandable. Later, in the 6th Dynasty, *Pepy I* calls himself "son of ***Hathor***," which seems reasonable since the king is considered to be the representative of ***Horus*** on earth. If ***Hathor*** is the mother of ***Horus***, the king becomes son of ***Hathor***.

In hieroglyphic writing, the name ***Hathor*** is read *"Hut Hor," "the home of Horus"* or the *"cosmic dwelling of Horus"* according to **Plutarch**. ***Hathor*** symbolizes the celestial space in which the solar ***Horus*** moves. As centuries go by, her cosmic functions are so expanded that she quickly becomes a universal goddess, a role she shares with ***Isis***. In fact, from the New Kingdom on, the two goddesses finally merge and adopt each other's iconography; in many cases, only the texts and legends can tell them apart. Very often, such a deity is displayed on the walls of tombs and temples: a woman wearing a crown with two horns stylized into a lyre, enclosing the solar disc. Is it ***Hathor*** or ***Isis***?

**The cow Hathor**

*The goddess Hathor has several iconographies: a woman crowned with stylized horns surrounding a solar disc, a woman with the head of a cow, or simply a cow. Of course, the choice of the representation depends on the function of the goddess the artist wanted to emphasize: the nurturing Hathor will be depicted as a cow; Hathor assimilated to Isis as protector of the dead will be depicted as a woman. Among the many personalities of this goddess, there is Hathor with the title of "Mistress of the Theban necropolis," and as such, she is often represented as a cow. Sometimes she appears coming out of a high mountain symbolizing the Libyan cliff where the tombs are dug and where the "Castles of Millions of Years" are located. In Deir el-Bahri, in her funerary temple, Hatshepsut reserved a special space for her. Sometimes she manifests herself as protector of the necropolis, sometimes she adopts the qualities of a cow nursing the future queen.*

Temple of Queen Hatshepsut
Deir el-Bahri,
New Kingdom,
West Thebes, Upper Egypt.

The answer to the question can only be given by reading the name of the deity, generally inscribed over her head. Sometimes the context gives an idea on the real identity of the goddess. For instance, if she appears with ***Osiris*** and ***Horus***, it is certainly ***Isis***. On the contrary, if she is depicted in a scene where she nurses the king, it can only be ***Hathor*** in her role as a nurturing deity.

The list of her attributions is very impressive: she is the goddess of love, lady of music, lady of **Byblos** and **Punt**, mistress of far lands, lady of the turquoise, lady of inebriation, mistress of ballets and gay songs… She nurses the royal child: in this case she is depicted as a woman or a cow feeding the young heir. She protects the necropolis of Thebes: she appears as a cow coming out of a high mountain symbolizing the Libyan cliff where the tombs are dug. She appears as goddess of dance, music and joy: she then has the aspect of a young woman waving a sistrum, which is a musical instrument that looks like a rattle, the sound of which is said to excite the gods. She is also lady of the sycamore in **Memphis**: in this case, she rises from a sycamore, which is a tree that feeds the souls of the deceased in the netherworld.

From an iconographical point of view, her most interesting appearance is the one where she is depicted as sovereign of the four corners of the sky and mistress of the cardinal points: she is represented on specific pillars, since they are crowned with "hathoric" capitals, with a cow's head engraved on each side. Each of these four faces symbolize a facet of her personality: ***Hathor*** the lioness as the eye of ***Re'*** slaying the enemies of the sun, ***Hathor*** the cow as goddess of love and rebirth, ***Hathor*** the cat as protector of homes and royal nurse, ***Hathor*** the cobra as the incarnation of beauty and youth.

Her main sanctuary is in **Dendara,** in Upper Egypt. The presently visible temple is the work of the last of the *Ptolemies* and several pharaohs of the Roman period, but if one is to believe the texts, this holy place goes back to the earliest times: it is very probable that the plan of the building was inspired from documents of the Old Kingdom, especially the reigns of *Khufu* and *Pepy I*. Every year, a celebration enlivened his part of Egypt: ***Hathor*** left her sanctuary in **Dendara** to visit her husband ***Horus Behedety***, a form of ***Horus*** worshipped in **Edfu**. This town is about ninety miles up the Nile.

For this trip, ***Hathor*** leaves her home for three weeks: the *"Mistress of Dandera is brought up the river, so that she can have a joyous reunion with **Horus**."* For this long trip, the solemn procession travels by river; the statue of ***Hathor*** is placed on a majestic boat, *"the Beautiful in Love,"* that sails up the Nile for four days. For its part, the clergy of **Edfu** makes preparations for the meeting of the spouses that is to happen outside the shrine, in a little chapel north of the town, at a very precise moment: the eighth hour of the day of the new moon of the eleventh month of the year. There ***Horus*** stands ready for his wife. As soon as she arrives, the festivities start, and the people living all around join in. She is acclaimed, she is greeted, her qualities are praised, music is played for her; she is ***Hathor*** *"the Golden," "the Lady of Goddesses," "the Mistress," "the Lady of inebriation, music and dance."* Then everyone gets into his own boat, and the procession makes for the main shrine. Once there, the priests pull the boats out of the water and bring them within the walls of the temple. ***Hathor*** makes the most of the occasion to see her father again, the sun, who manifests himself in **Edfu** by the side of ***Horus Behedety***. The ancient texts present Hathor as the uraeus, one of the manifestations of the solar eye, and explain how here *"she meets her father **Re'**, who exults to see her, for it is his eye that is back."* The mythical wedding can at last take place; it is accompanied by great rejoicing, at the end of which the two spouses are left alone together for their wedding night. The festivities in **Edfu** really start the next day, and they last the fourteen days of the crescent moon. Fourteen days during which rites, sacrifices, commemorations, visits to the shrine take place... The priests specifically organize a set of ceremonies for the divine souls and *"the gods that died in Edfu."* These are the primeval gods, created by the demiurge to assist him in his creation, but called to disappear after the creation. It is said that *"their souls flew to heaven, where they live amongst the stars,"* and that *"the necropolis of Edfu contains the bodies of those ancestral gods."* Every year, *"**Re'** goes there, accompanied by the Majesty of his uraeus (**Hathor**); he takes care of his children, the divine and respectable bodies who rest forever in Edfu, leaves them offerings and listens to their prayers."* The festivities end with a great banquet at the end of which each goes back to his own sanctuary: ***Hathor*** to **Dendara** and ***Horus*** to **Edfu**.

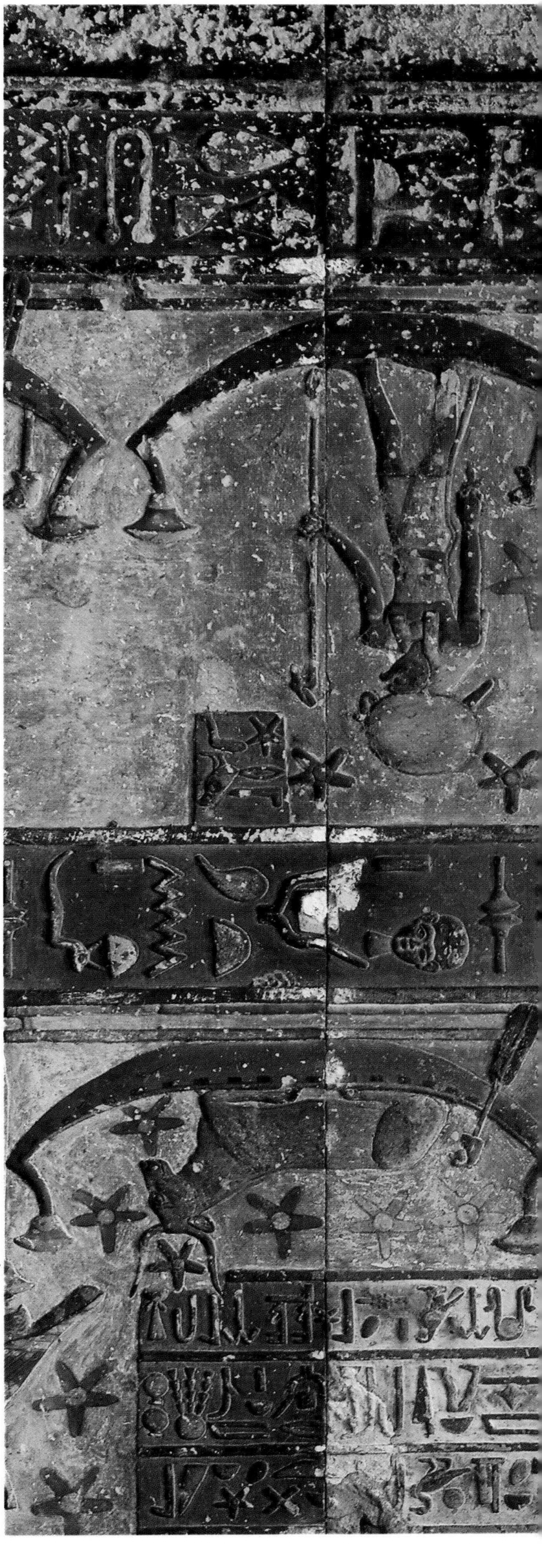

**Hathor in Dendara**

*The ceiling of the hypostyle hall of Hathor's temple in Dendara is decorated with scenes of astronomy that are most original. Hours of the day and of the night, celestial regions, decades, gods of the cardinal points, the constellations are represented. Here, on the south side, there is a scene that is found in several other places of the shrine, that pictures Nut, the canopy of heaven. Her body is covered with the waters of the lower ocean and stretches from one end to the other of the room; her feet lie to the east and her head to the west. When the sun god goes through his cyclical trip, he uses alternatively Nut's daily and nightly bodies: during the day, he shines on the earth; in the evening he is swallowed by the goddess and disappears to shine on the underground regions. In the morning he is born back on earth and, thus regenerated, he can start a new trip through the day. Here we see the birth of the sun shining with a lot of rays on the temple of Dendara, which is symbolized by a building crowned by the cow's head of Hathor.*

Temple of Hathor,
Ptolemaic Period,
Dendara, Upper Egypt.

## Harakhty

Harakhty 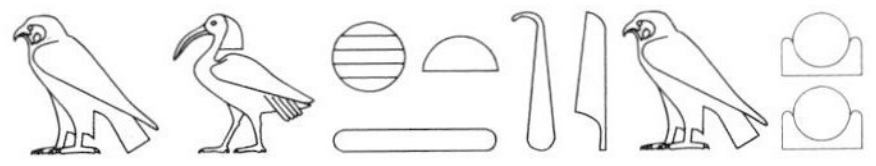

"Horus of the Horizon"

Creative god in Heliopolis, the incarnation of the sun at its zenith under the name of Re'-Harakhty

Principal place of worship: Heliopolis (Lower Egypt)

Representation: a man with the head of a falcon or a falcon crowned with a solar disc

His name means "***Horus*** of the Horizon" and he represents one of the diurnal forms of the sun god in **Heliopolis**. In this very ancient tradition, ***Re'*** takes on personalities and representations that change during his trip through the sky. In the morning, he is ***Khepri***, the rising sun; he is depicted as a beetle. At its zenith, he becomes ***Re'-Harakhty***, and takes the image of a falcon by assuming the personalities of the sun ***Re'***, and of the falcon of the horizon, ***Harakhty***. In the evening he becomes ***Atum***, the setting sun, represented as an old man. ***Harakhty,*** there, is the symbol of the sun in all its

glory, that shines upon the organized world: *"the one that reigns beyond time and space."* That is why very often the texts indifferently use the names of ***Re'-Harakhty***, ***Harakhty*** or ***Re'*** to designate this supreme deity, who is generally called "the Universal Master" in the myths and in the legends.

His symbolic representation reminds us of his two main qualities. He is shown as a man with the head of a hawk, or sometimes simply as a hawk crowned with a great solar disc. The falcon symbolizes his celestial features; the disc his solar personality.

In the temple of ***Horus*** in **Edfu**, the inner walls recall the tales of the battles ***Horus*** led against the enemies of ***Re'***. The text stipulates the exact name of the protagonists: they are ***Horus Behedety***, particularly venerated in Upper Egypt, in **Edfu**, as solar and royal god, and ***Re'-Harakhty***, the victorious sun. Of course, this legend could have been interpreted the same way if the scribe had just mentioned simply ***Horus*** and ***Re'***. But if these details appear it is because they are really important: we are in **Edfu**, where ***Horus Behedety*** is worshipped and he is a particular form of ***Horus***. Therefore, it is natural that local myths should show divine personalities that have a direct relationship with the local cult.

We are *"in the year 363 of his Majesty, the King of Upper and Lower Egypt, **Re'-Harakhty**."* The king of gods is in **Nubia** to contemplate his creation. But during this short routine visit, he learns that there is a conspiracy against him. Of course, amongst the plotters are the henchmen of ***Apophis***, the cosmic enemy who never ceases to attack the solar vessel to impede the correct progress of the universe. ***Re'-Harakhty*** immediately has his son ***Horus Behedety*** called for, and asks him to get rid of his enemies. The first battle is a great victory for ***Horus Behedety***. But the conspirators retreat and move to Egypt. ***Horus Behedety*** persecutes them all the way up to the Delta of the Nile, winning battle after battle. But the war never ceases, because each time the enemies reappear under other forms: they take the forms of ***Seth*** or ***Apophis***, and turn into hippopotami or crocodiles. In the end, ***Horus Behedety*** manages to push them back all the way to the Red Sea, beyond the borders of Egypt. He even makes them find refuge in foreign and hostile Asian countries. ***Thoth*** and ***Re'-Harakhty*** congratulate him vigorously, and everyone goes back to his own home: ***Re'-Harakhty*** goes back to **Nubia** and ***Horus Behedety*** reinstates his temple in **Edfu**.

It seems obvious that the elaboration of this myth by the clergy of ***Horus Behedety*** in **Edfu** is an answer to a religious necessity. In these few words, the god of the town is given a direct filiation to the king of gods: in this legend, ***Horus Behedety*** is the son of ***Re'-Harakhty***. Besides, he is given the leading part in the fight between the cosmic enemies and in the keeping of the order of the universe.

**The sun boat**

*There are several themes that appear in this scene painted on the Tanethereret sarcophagus. To the right, the deceased woman is wearing a white linen dress and is playing the sistrum, an activity particularly reserved to women, to several gods that are facing her. In the middle, sails the solar boat with Ma'at, the goddess of justice and truth wearing an ostrich's feather, Thoth, the baboon, and Re', the sun, sheltered by a canopy. He is holding in his hands the insignia of royalty: the was scepter, the flail, and the cross of life. The boat is set upon a black band with pointed ends, which is the stylized hieroglyphic sign to designate the sky. Underneath appears the image of the snake Apophis. He regularly appears from the chaos with the sole object of attacking and overturning the solar boat. He is incessantly pushed back to the end of the world by the defenders of the sun: this fight without end illustrates the victory of the created world over the forces of chaos. In the foreground, four dogs seem to pull the boat: they represent Anubis, the god of embalmers.*

Third Intermediary Period.

## *Horus*

Horus 

Son of Osiris and Isis

Husband of Hathor (sometimes son of Hathor)

Deity with several functions: celestial and solar god, direct protector of Egyptian royalty, representative of the gods on earth

Other deities assimilated to Horus: Harakhty, Harmakhis, Haroeris, Hurun, Harpokrates, Harsiese

Principal place of worship: Edfu (Upper Egypt)

Representation: a falcon or a man with a falcon's head

Many deities are represented as falcons in the Egyptian pantheon. The most famous one is ***Horus***, who is several gods in one. First of all, he is a celestial god who has a close relationship with the solar god and reigns over the sky and the stars. He takes on the personalities of several gods, who are equally presented under the form of a falcon: ***Harakhty***, ***Harmakhis***, ***Haroeris***, ***Hurun***... After the unification of Egypt under the kings of **Hierakonpolis**, the falcon god of this town becomes of course the royal god: he is the protector of the king, who himself is considered to be the incarnation of ***Horus*** on earth. He is also member of the cosmogony of **Heliopolis**, as he is the son of ***Isis*** and ***Osiris,*** and so he includes deities linked through this kinship: ***Harpokrates***, ***Harsomtus***, ***Harsiese***... Through the centuries, all these personalities will merge into one divinity that stems from all these mythological streams.

The mythological texts tell us how, after ***Osiris*** had been killed by his brother ***Seth***, ***Isis*** succeeds in conceiving a child, the future ***Horus***, from her dead husband. That being done without the killer's knowledge, ***Isis*** is afraid for her life and the one of the son she carries in her womb. So she implores the creative god, ***Re'-Atum*** to protect her from eventual attacks from ***Seth***. Then comes the much-awaited day of the birth:

*"I am **Horus**, the great falcon... My place is far from **Seth**'s place, the enemy of my father **Osiris**. I have reached the roads of eternity and light. I fly away thanks to my launch. No god can do what I have done. I shall fight the enemy of my father **Osiris**, I shall put him under my sandals in my name of Furious... For I am **Horus**, whose place is far from gods and men. I am **Horus**, the son of **Isis**."*

The tales about the travels of ***Isis*** and the childhood of ***Horus*** are numerous. It is clear that of all the gods, little ***Horus*** is the one most inclined to fall sick and to have accidents. As a prototype of the weak, unshielded, sickly, helpless, innocent and vulnerable child, he is spared absolutely nothing: scorpion bites, intestinal aches, unexplained fevers, indigestion, mutilations... But the power of magic and the intervention of the gods always put an end to his sufferings.

One of the most well known extracts takes us to the marshes of the Delta, close to the town of **Chemnis**. It's a hostile region, and ***Isis*** knows that ***Seth*** will never venture into this desert. She therefore feels safe, but the days are long and difficult. She has to beg to subsist. In the morning, she hides her son and disguises herself as a beggar woman to go throughout the country and look for food.

One evening, she finds the young ***Horus*** completely unconscious. In spite of a ravenous hunger, he is so weak that he cannot suck his mother's breast. ***Isis*** calls in the people living in the marshes who try to help her, but unfortunately without success. Then an old woman, famous for her gift of magic, comes along. She declares that the ailment the baby is suffering from does not come from his uncle ***Seth***. ***Horus*** has simply been bitten, she says, by a scorpion or a snake. ***Isis*** looks closer, and sees that he has indeed been poisoned. Then ***Nephthys*** and ***Serket***, the scorpion goddess, arrive. They advise ***Isis*** to ask ***Re'*** to stop his course until ***Horus*** gets better. When he hears her prayer, the solar god sends ***Thoth*** to ***Isis***. He looks at the child and says:

*"Don't worry **Isis**! I've come to you, armed with the vital breath that will heal the child. Courage, **Horus**! The one who lives in the solar disc protects you, and your protection is eternal. Out! Poison. **Re'**, the great god will make you disappear. The sun boat stopped, and will only resume is course once you're healed. The wells will be empty, the crops will fail, the men will be deprived of bread until **Horus** has his strength back for his mother's happiness. Courage, **Horus**. The poison is dead, it has been vanquished."*

### The Horus name

*The stela of the "snake king" is the name given to a great slab of stone found in the necropolis of Abydos, that shelters the royal tombs of the thinite period. Most likely, Snake is the fourth pharaoh of the first dynasty: Egypt has just entered its historical phase, and writing is still very succinct. However, the skillfulness of the carving of this slab is surprising, because the art of stone-carving is at its beginning. This work shows the masterful art of the carver who puts many details into the finishing touches: the scales of the snake, the wings of the hawk and the façade of the palace are examples which allow us to appreciate his work. In the stela appears King Djet's (the Snake king) Horus name which is the first name of Pharaoh in his royal titles. The king is considered to be the incarnation of the hawk Horus who protects him and helps him in all circumstances.*

Thinite Period.

The poison having been thrown off by the great magician, young ***Horus*** comes back to life. ***Thoth***, after having asked the inhabitants of **Chemnis** to look after the child in the absence of his mother, leaves the scene of the accident, in order to *"set the sun boat back on its course, and to announce to **Re'** that **Horus** is well again and the poison defeated."*

In the struggle that opposes him to ***Seth***, he is often subject to mutilations, which each time are repaired thanks to his own powers. Nothing can hurt the inner part of a god; only a part of his potential strength can be affected. Certain accounts of the myth offer details on the episode when ***Seth*** invites ***Horus*** to his home, with the intention of laying a trap for him. The story tells how, after dinner, ***Seth*** tries to abuse ***Horus***. But ***Horus***, aware of the danger, manages to collect the sperm of his enemy in his hands. He goes back to ***Isis*** who, panic-stricken, cuts his hands off and throws them in the water. Wanting never to see them again, she uses her most powerful magic to sink them in the mud and prevent them from ever being replaced on her son's body. Handicapped of course, ***Horus*** askes help from the

Universal Master who, understanding how annoying the situation is, sends the crocodile god ***Sobek*** to retrieve the lost hands. But since the accident the hands have become completely independent, and are very difficult to catch. They have incarnated ever since two of the sons of ***Horus***. In the end ***Sobek*** retrieves the hands with a net, and gives them to the Universal Master, who decides to duplicate them, wanting to avoid any trouble: to satisfy ***Isis***, he offers the first pair as a relic to the holy town of Nekhen and to free ***Horus***, he gives him back the second pair.

## *Hurun*

Hurun 

*Solar god assimilated to the sphinx of Giza (Harmakhis)*
*Principal place of worship: Giza (Lower Egypt)*
*Representation: falcon or sphinx*

Of Canaanite origin, ***Hurun*** is worshipped in Egypt from the New Kingdom onwards. He is known for his particular effectiveness in the fight against evil, but it's mainly because of his assimilation to ***Harmakhis***, and as such to the sphinx of **Giza**, that his cult goes into Lower Egypt. A small shrine is consecrated to him north of the great sphinx as early as the 18th Dynasty, under the reign of *Amenhotep II*: he becomes *"**Hurun**, the great god, the lord of heaven."* Some scribes even use the name ***Hurun-Harmakhis*** to designate the sphinx of **Giza**, translating a perfect merging of both gods. This association is so strong that very soon ***Hurun*** assumes ***Harmakhis***'s personality: he acquires solar characteristics and is assimilated to ***Horus***, since the name ***Harmakhis*** means "***Horus*** on the Horizon."

The iconography of ***Hurun*** recalls his double origin: sometimes he is a sphinx and sometimes a falcon. But in fact, his cult hardly goes further than the site of **Giza**. His part in the royal ideology is very limited, and in contrast to other Asian deities imported into Egypt, ***Baal*** and ***Reshep*** for instance, he never appears next to the pharaoh in scenes of war. He is mainly worshipped by common people and within the **Giza** area. There are a few documents that discretly mention him in other parts of the country: in **Deir el-Medina** (Upper Egypt, West Thebes) or in the eastern part of the Delta. But they are rare and isolated.

On the other hand, he appears as a victorious hero in the **Harris Papyrus**. The story recounts how the gods, called upon to protect ***Horus*** against wild animals, work together to stop a wolf: ***Hurun*** does not care about its threats, for he is helped by ***Herishef*** who *"cuts its leg,"* by ***Anta*** who *"massacres"* it and by ***Horus*** who takes a weapon with which ***Seth*** kills the animal. The victory is considered to be that of the god ***Hurun***, *"the victorious shepherd."* Here he plays the part that is given to great Asiatic gods, and intervenes to keep away everything that is bad for man.

**Hemen represented as the falcon Horus**

*There are many deities that are represented as hawks. Very often, they have a direct relationship to Horus, and incarnate a particular aspect of his personality: this is true for Harakhty, Harmakhis, Hurun, Harsomtus, Haroeris, Harsiese and Harpokrates. It is also true for Hemen. Very few things are known about this god, except that he is the patron of the town of Mo'alla, in Upper Egypt, and that he appeared under the form of the falcon Horus. This statuary group represents Taharqa, a pharaoh of the 25th Dynasty, offering two vessels of wine to Hurun the falcon god. It is probably an ex-voto. This kind of offering is made to thank the gods for their beneficent intervention in human life: a good flooding of the Nile, the healing of somebody sick, a victory in battle... The work is made from a rather surprising assembly of materials: the wood pedestal is covered with a thick layer of silver plating; the statuette of the hawk in schist is covered with sheets of gold, and Taharqa is made out of bronze.*
Third Intermediary Period.

## Isis

Isis 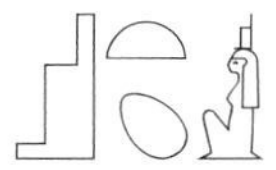

*Daughter of Geb, the earth, and Nut, the sky*

*Wife and sister of Osiris*

*Universal goddess with many roles, who acts in all circumstances, in the world of the living as well as in the other world*

*Principal place of worship: Philae (Upper Egypt)*

*Representation: a woman with a high back seat on her head*

No other figure in the Egyptian pantheon can rival the goddess ***Isis***. She is so popular that few spheres are out of her reach. Her image is everywhere, from the big sanctuaries of the Nile Valley to the smallest tokens of private faith. She belongs to the great Ennead of **Heliopolis**, where she appears as the daughter of ***Geb*** and ***Nut***, and especially as the sister and wife of ***Osiris***. In fact, her tremendous popularity comes from her irreproachable attitude in the Osirian mythology, where she is credited with being a faithful spouse and devoted mother. She is the one who goes and looks for her husband murdered by ***Seth***. She is the one who puts together the pieces of his body and brings him back to life. She is the one again who secretly rears little ***Horus*** who is destined to ascend to the throne of Egypt. She thus becomes the protector of women and children. The reputation of her magic increases the number of her faithful: she knows how to extract the poison from a bite, to drive out evil, to banish sickness, and even her words, it is said, *"are capable of giving life back to those choking their last breath."* Her funerary role is also essential: as she is directly responsible for giving life back to ***Osiris***, she is given the role of protector of the deceased. Her emblem is the magic knot, an amulet in the form of the cross of life, the two branches bending downwards to symbolize protection.

***Isis*** doesn't have any specific representations, but she is generally portrayed as a woman with a throne on her head, which is a hieroglyphic sign used to write her name. Over the centuries, she has assumed the personalities of many feminine divinities. In these cases, she borrows their particular iconography: she is the cow ***Hathor***, the lioness ***Sakhmet***, the scorpion ***Serket***, or carries the attributes belonging to ***Neith***, ***Satis***, ***Opet***, ***Renenutet***...

Under the Ptolemaic and Roman dynasties, she became the universal goddess, and her cult spread far beyond Egypt's boundaries. The *"sovereign of all gods"* accumulates all kinds of capabilities. She is goddess of the dead, and protector of life in the other world; she is synonymous with beautiful harvests and watches over households; she protects the royal function and ensures the balance of the universe.

In the Roman Empire, she lasted for an extraordinarily long time: her temple in **Philae** is shut in 551, under the reign of Emperor *Justinian*. It is the end of the Egyptian pagan cult. This is why it is very difficult to describe the personality of this goddess, who appears in a great many legends and myths, and who is portrayed in almost all the pharaonic sanctuaries, including those which are not entirely devoted to her.

In many cases the legends present gods who are subject to human passions and feelings that reflect the instability and vulnerability inherent to human beings. Here ***Isis*** embodies women's curiosity and natural mischievousness (they are supposedly capable of the most dire intrigues to have their way).

The tale starts with an apologia of the Universal Master, the solar god ***Re'***, who is at the source of all life, and whose power has no end. His force is such that he can appear under any aspect. His names are so many and so secret that no one knows them all. Of course, all this attracts ***Isis***'s jealousy, who would like to usurp his power, and become, in his place, the mistress of the world. So she sets about to discover the secret name of ***Re'***: she thinks that its knowledge will allow her to overpower him. To do this, she watches the comings and goings of the solar god in the sky, and notices with amazement how old he has become: he even drools on the ground. She picks up some of the saliva, mixes it with some earth, and with this clay, molds a snake in the shape of an arrow, that she leaves by a crossing that is used by the solar procession. Soon after, the procession comes to the crossing, and the snake, animated by Isis from afar, bites with all its might the flesh of ***Re'*** who lets out a scream and falls down, terribly weakened. His lips tremble and his body is racked with spasms: the poison is taking possession of his body. He manages to collect his strength to call for help and to tell his sorry story to the gods. He even feels obliged to explain the reasons for his secret name.

**The goddess Isis**

*Isis is one of the protectors of the deceased in the Underworld, due to the part she plays in the "Legend of Osiris." It is told that after her husband has been dismembered by Seth, she leaves with her sister Nephthys to look for all the pieces that have been strewn across Egypt. Once this had been done, she asks Anubis to assist her, and the two of them create the first mummy. In the same way, she has looked after Osiris, she watches over the deceased, and participates in his resurrection. This is why she appears at the head and Nephthys at the foot of the sarcophagi. The granite coffin of Ramesses III shows this style of iconography: here, Isis, with her emblem on her head, stretches out her wings to protect the deceased. She is kneeling on the sign of gold, which is considered to be the "flesh of the gods." At her side, two jackals ensure the king the preservation of his body, since they symbolize Anubis, patron of the embalmers.*

New Kingdom.

And ***Re'*** explained: "*My father and my mother taught me my name, and I hid it within my body so that no magician could throw a spell on me. Just now I was setting out to contemplate my creation when something I don't know bit me. It is neither fire, nor water; but my heart is in flames, my body shivers and my limbs are cold. Bring me my children, those who know the magic formulas and whose science reaches the sky.*" The divinities rush to his side, and amongst them is ***Isis*** with all her magic. She wonders: "*What is this? Has one of your children set himself against you? In that case, I shall destroy him with my magic and I shall banish him from your sight.*" ***Re'*** explains to her the nature of his ailment. And ***Isis*** answers: "*Tell me your name, divine father! For a man can only come back to life when he has been called by his name.*" The solar god tells her all his names, but in vain, for the poison keeps on acting. "*Your name is not amongst the ones you told me. Tell it to me and the poison will leave your body, for a man revives when his name is pronounced*" repeats ***Isis***. And ***Re'***, overcome with pain, finally gives her his secret: "*Listen to me, daughter* ***Isis,*** *so that my name goes from my body into yours... When it leaves my heart, repeat it to your son* ***Horus*** *and bind him with a divine oath.*" Having heard her father's name, ***Isis*** delivers him from the poison.

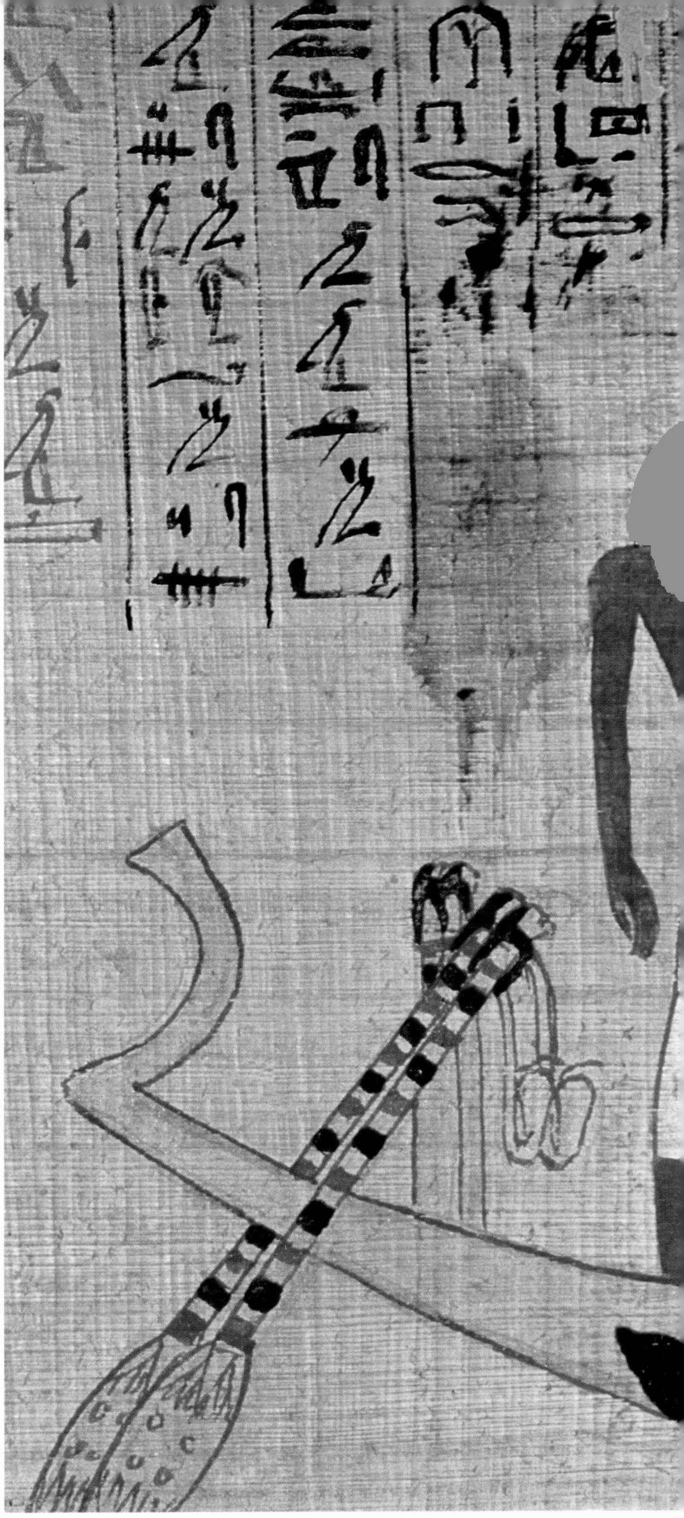

## *Khepri*

Khepri 

Creative god in Heliopolis incarnating the rising sun
Principal place of worship: Heliopolis (Lower Egypt)
Representation: a beetle or man with the head of a beetle

***Khepri*** is the form the sun adopts at dawn. In hieroglyphic writing, his name has just one sign, the beetle, which belongs to the group of triliteral signs. This term is used for a sign representing three consonants, or semi-consonants: here *hpr*, or **kheper** if the vowels are pronounced. The precise translation of the word is still difficult to give. Literally, one could translate it by *"coming to existence,"* to *"become,"* or to *"be."* Whatever its real signification, it expresses an idea of birth, transformation and becoming. By deduction, the god ***Khepri*** shall be understood as *"the one who came into existence by himself."* And the cosmogony of **Heliopolis** relates very precisely the origins of this solar god: he emerged from the primeval ocean, ***Nun***, and fashioned a physical body for himself. He has neither father nor mother: he is his own creator. He is at the same time ***Khepri***, ***Re'*** and ***Atum***: the sun at dawn, the sun at its zenith, and the setting sun. Thus ***Khepri*** is always pictured as a beetle. Sometimes he is depicted as a man holding a beetle over his head, or more rarely, a man with the head of a beetle.

It seems quite obvious that the representation of ***Khepri*** is an analogy between the behavior of the beetle and that of the sun. According to **Plutarch**, these animals have no female representative; they *"put their semen into a kind of matter that they turn into a ball*

**Khepri**
*The sun adopts different symbols and names according to the time of the day it is represented. At dawn, it is Khepri, "the one that comes to existence," and it is depicted as a beetle. At its zenith, it becomes Re' and is described as a solar disc. At dusk, it is Atum, and becomes an old man, or a man with a ram's head. On this vignette from the Imenemsaf Papyrus, the god represented in the celestial boat is the rising sun. However, the artist has chosen the unusual iconography of a man with the head of a beetle: in most cases, it is the simple representation of a beetle that evoques Khepri.*
Late Period.

*which they roll by pushing it with their hind legs."* Then they hide it in long underground galleries so that the little coleopter can be born protected from exterior aggressions. The ball they push describes, in a figurative fashion, the course of the sun in the sky; the burying of the eggs and the birth of the young beetle, coming out of hiding, symbolize the daily rejuvenation of the sun after its nightly journey.

In the tombs of the **Valley of the Kings** there are many scenes that recall the voyages of the sun. These illustrated texts, called "**cosmographies**," describe the nightly journey of ***Re'*** in the infernal regions of the Underworld in very detailed manner. The most astonishing, as well as the oldest, of all these compositions about **Tuat**, the world below, is called the "**Book of What is in the Tuat**". The twelve hours of the night are organized as regions crossed by a river, the underground Nile. The sun boat floats on this river, with the god ***Re'***, his attendants and the deceased king on board.

On its banks, hundreds of deceased inhabitants of the **Tuat** stand by to acclaim the sun god. The retinue crosses the twelve subterranean regions, where obstacles or cosmic enemies are there to constantly impede its long journey. In particular, ***Apophis***, the giant malignant snake, constantly attacks the divine bark with the intention of overturning it. But each time he is sent back to chaos. At last, at dawn, the god ***Re'*** appears triumphantly in the shape of ***Khepri***, the sun reborn. He can then start his diurnal trip.

# *Khnum*

Khnum 

*Associated with Neith (Esna), and with Satis and Anukis (Elephantine)*

*Deity of creation (Esna); patron of the cataract and guardian of the sources of the Nile (Elephantine)*

*Places of worship: Esna and Elephantine (Upper Egypt)*

*Representation: a ram or a man with the head of a ram*

***Khnum*** is the potter god with a ram's head venerated for his multiple functions in many towns of Egypt. His two main places of worship are in **Esna**, where he is the demiurge next to the goddess ***Neith***, and in **Elephantine**, where he is the guardian of the sources of the Nile with ***Satis*** and ***Anukis***.

***Khnum*** is the local god of **Elephantine**, an island situated north of the first cataract, and on the southern border of Egypt. It is here that the Nile enters the Egyptian territory. Everyone knows the importance the Nile has for the ancient Egyptians, who knew nothing, however, about its sources or the origin of the flood. Thus ***Khnum*** is designated as the guardian of the sources of the Nile, patron of the first cataract, and master of the mythical caves which are supposed to spout the nutritious waters. In his Elephantine sanctuary, where he is honored with his wife ***Satis*** and the infant goddess ***Anukis***, he receives a very popular following. Egyptians came from all over the country with offerings and presents for him, as it is he, ***Khnum,*** who decides how much silt is to be set free during the flood. An inscription on the island of Sehel recalls this domination of the ram god over the Nile waters: *"There is a town in the midst of the water; the Nile surrounds it. It's called* ***Elephantine****. It's the beginning of the beginning...* ***Khnum*** *sits there as god, his sandals on the water; he holds the lock of the door in his hand and opens the doors according to his will."* Then, as he has the power to let the silt flow or not on the land of Egypt, so he is a giver of life, hence a creative god.

The personality of the god ***Khnum*** has become more familiar to us since the texts of his temple in **Esna** have been translated. We already knew about his role as a potter, thanks to narratives that recall the divine birth of certain pharaohs; he fashioned on his wheel the image of the royal child, as well as his **ka,** which is more or less his vital energy. A very famous tale, that we know thanks to the **Westcar papyrus**, tells how **Redjedjet**, wife of the priest of ***Re'***, **Rauser**, gave birth to the first three kings of the 5th Dynasty. For this unusual delivery, ***Khnum*** and the goddesses ***Isis***, ***Nephthys***, ***Meskhenet*** and ***Heqet*** play their part:

*"Then* ***Isis*** *stood in front of her,* ***Nephthys*** *behind her and* ***Heqet*** *hurried the birth. And* ***Isis*** *said: «Do not be too strong in her womb, in your name* ***Userkaf****.» The child then slipped into her hands: it was a child, long as a cubit, with strong bones. His limbs were inlaid with gold and he wore a real lapis lazuli headdress. They washed him once his umbilical cord had been cut and placed him into a brick frame. Then* ***Meskhenet*** *went up to him and said: «a sovereign who will reign over the whole country,» while* ***Khnum*** *put health into his body."*

In the same way, during the 18th Dynasty, Queen *Hatshepsut* decided to represent this divine filiation on the walls of her funerary temple in **Deir el-Bahri**. The scene shows how the god ***Amun***, as *Tuthmosis I*, comes to mate with Queen *Ahmes* in order to conceive little *Hatshepsut*. Depicted behind, are the potter god ***Khnum***, shaping the body and the **ka** of the little princess, his assistant ***Heqet***, the frog goddess, and the group of the seven **Hathor**.

Later documents, mainly those of the temple of **Esna**, extend ***Khnum***'s creative activity to the gods, men and human species. He becomes the demiurge who molded on his potter's wheel the primeval egg from which the sun sprang forth at the beginning of time. The **Esna** texts are interesting for several reasons: they not only enlighten us on ***Khnum***'s personality as creator, but they also reveal the persistence of the Egyptian religion during the Greco-Roman period. Most of these texts date back to the reigns of *Trajan* and *Hadrian,* Roman emperors of the 2nd century A.D. They are the most recent texts we have from the pharaonic period. They are an ingenious synthesis of beliefs: a mixture of ritual texts and prayers, hymns and litanies, tales of creation and others. The theologians here needed to be clever to write the theogonic texts, since the temple is dedicated to two creative divinities: ***Khnum*** and ***Neith*** (the archer of the town of **Sais**, known also as the primordial cow ***Ihet***).

**The ram Khnum**

*Khnum is a god worshipped in several parts of Upper Egypt. In Elephantine, he watches over the sources of the Nile, and is given the title of "Lord of the cataract." In Esna, he has the role of creative god, and shapes the world on his potter's wheel. Like many other deities incarnated by an animal, the ram of Khnum also has the benefit of its own religion: it is considered a sacred animal. It gets special attention during its life; after it dies, it is mummified and buried according to rites similar to those of human beings. On the island of Elephantine, facing Aswan, Khnum has a sanctuary that today is in ruins, close to which there is a necropolis of sacred rams. The wooden coffins are enriched with different ornaments: gold leaf plating, collages of stuccoed fabric, and gold paint...*
Late Period.

The cosmogonic texts of **Esna** are unusual. No detail about the creation has been forgotten by the theologians. One learns that ***Khnum*** moulded all the gods and men on his wheel, working in his shop *"with the action of his arms."* He also modeled the livestock, the herds, the fish, the birds, the reproductive males and the females. The text follows with a methodical description of all the aspects of the human physiognomy: *"he made the hair and the locks grow. He shaped the skin on the limbs. He built the skull and moulded the face so as to give it the characteristic aspect of faces. He opened the eyes and the ears. He put the body in close contact with the atmosphere. He made the mouth to eat, and teeth to chew. He also untied the tongue so that it could speak. He made the throat so that it could swallow and also spit..."* And all the parts of the body are described in this fashion: the throat, the spine, the bladder, the internal organs, the heart... The conclusion is clear: *"all the beings were moulded on his wheel."*

Another excerpt extends his capacity for creation beyond the Valley of the Nile, since he *"created all the exotic products from the other lands so that the tributes could be given to the foreign countries,"* that is, to Egypt. The text finishes with the conception of the elements of nature: *"In the country, he gave life to the plants. He covered the riverbanks with flowers. He made it so the trees of life yielded their fruit as food for men and gods. He opened faults on the body of the mountains, and made the quarries spurt their stones."*

The end of the hymn gives a general survey of ***Khnum***'s part in creation: *"He always comes at the right moment... Children's destiny and growth follow what he orders. The water and the wind obey him and what he demands is immediately done. This and that, it is he who made everything, for nothing can be accomplished without him."*

His double role as creative god and guardian of the sources of the Nile, makes him a very popular Egyptian god. He appears in tombs and in temples next to the king and the great gods as a man with the head of a ram. His powers are so extensive that he can intervene at any time. It is said for instance that he can annihilate the snake ***Apophis*** and his descendants, but it is also he who is in charge of cleaning the pharaoh of all impurities during the jubilee and coronation festivities.

## *Khons*

Khons

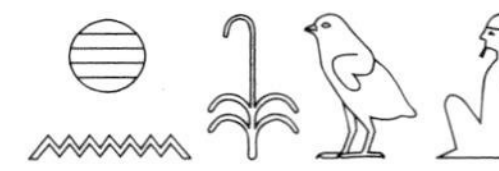

*Associated in a triad with the god Amun and the goddess Mut*

*Moon god*

*Principal place of worship: Karnak / Luxor (Upper Egypt)*

*Representation: mummified man, man with a hawk's head or young lad wearing the lock of youth and a moon crescent on his head*

His name means "the Wanderer," "the Traveller," or, according to the texts in the temple of **Edfu**, *"the One who crosses"* the sky. ***Khons*** is by nature a travelling god, as he's in direct relation with the moon: he is, after ***Thoth***, the most important lunar god in the Egyptian pantheon. He probably first appears during the Old Kingdom, as his name is quoted in the "**Pyramid Texts**" of *King Unas*, the last pharaoh of the 5th Dynasty. However, apart from this one example, he is rarely mentioned in the documents of this very ancient period. He must have been at that time a local lunar god without any particular influence. His cult flourishes during the New Kingdom. He becomes the god-son of the Theban triad: he is associated with the god of the Kingdom, ***Amun***, and with his consort ***Mut***. For several centuries the three of them rule the Egyptian religious scenery. Their association allows the Theban clergy to constitute a divine family, which concentrates the three vital principles of all creation: a solar god, ***Amun-Re'***, a celestial goddess, ***Mut***, and a moon god, ***Khons***. There is a shrine devoted to ***Khons*** in ***Amun's*** sanctuary in **Karnak.** But the most interesting reliefs that concern him are in ***Mut***'s sacred precinct, in what is left of an ancient temple from the New Kingdom, and today badly destroyed scenes carved on the walls recall the birth, circumcision and childhood of the god ***Khons***.

The iconography of ***Khons*** recalls the two essential features of his personality: he is at the same time a moon god and a child god. So he is depicted as a man with mummy wrappings wearing a moon disc on his head; and instead of hair or a wig, he wears a lock of hair on his right temple. This characteristic sign, worn by every child whether god or mortal, is called the *"lock of youth"* and is there to indicate the youth of the represented boy.

**The god-son Khons**

*Khons is a deity closely related to the moon, associated from the New Kingdom with Amun, the god of the Kingdom, and his consort Mut. The representation of Khons takes into account this double characteristic: as a lunar god, he wears a headdress that contains a moon crescent and a solar disc; and as a child god, he wears the lock of infancy, a lock of hair at times plaited, on his right temple. The royal cobra, the uraeus, rears up on his brow, and Khons holds in his hands a sistrum. This relief, carved in a beautiful piece of pink granite, is called a "sunken relief"; this technique consists of carving the image into the stone, so that once the work is finished, the surface of the stone appears in the foreground. In a different technique, bas-relief, the artist will carve the stone all around his main subject, so that it will appear flat. In the latter case, the motif, not the surface of the stone, will appear in the foreground.*

New Kingdom.

# *THE WEIGHING OF THE SOUL ON A*

***OSIRIS***
*GOD OF THE DEAD*

***THE "GREAT EATER"***
*HAS TO DEVOUR THE DEAD'S SOUL*
*IF THE JUDGMENT IS UNFAVORABLE*

***ABOVE, THE FORTY-TWO DEITIES OF THE JUDGMENT HALLS***

# PAPYRUS FROM THE PTOLEMAIC PERIOD

**THOTH**
INSCRIBES THE OUTCOME OF THE JUDGMENT

**ANUBIS**
GOD OF EMBALMERS

**HORUS**
IN CHARGE OF THE WEIGHING WITH ANUBIS

**THE DECEASED AND MA'AT**
GODDESS OF TRUTH AND JUSTICE

HAVE TO HELP OSIRIS IN JUDGING THE DECEASED

*Previous pages*

**Ma'at and the deceased**

*This papyrus, finely drawn in pen and ink, portrays the traditional weighing of the soul. The deceased is ushered into the Judgment Halls by the goddess Ma'at, whose head has been replaced by her emblem, the ostrich feather. Close to the balance, Horus with the head of a hawk, and Anubis, with the head of a jackal, check the weighing while Thoth, with the head of an ibis, waits for the verdict to be pronounced so that he can inscribe it on his tablets. In front, the "Great Eater" sitting on a pedestal, stays ready to devour the heart if it doesn't manage to balance with the feather. The Eater impatiently looks at Osiris, the Lord of the tribunal, sitting on a canopy. At the top, close to each other, are the forty two mortuary deities who have to judge the deceased.*
Ptolemaic Period.

**The god Min**

*Min has a very particular iconography, in direct relation to his function, as he is god of fertility and reproduction. He is swaddled as a mummy, with an erect penis. His right arm, squarely lifted high behind his head, carries the flail, which is a royal and divine insignia. His crown is the same as Amun's, with a solar disc leaning against two tall feathers above a mortier. In fact, Min is considered to be a hypostasis of Amun; in hieroglyphic signs, their names are written the same way. It is to be understood that, Amun, god of the Kingdom, manifests his fecund, fertilizing and creative qualities in the guise of Min, who only represents one of his many facets.*
Late Period.

# *Ma'at*

Ma'at 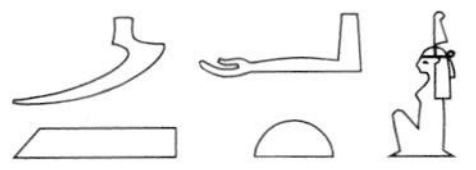

Daughter of Re'

Goddess of justice and truth

Representation: an ostrich feather or a woman wearing an ostrich feather on her head

***Ma'at*** is considered to be the daughter of ***Re'***, and she personifies truth and justice, universal order and cosmic equilibrium needed at the time of the creation. Thanks to her, the organized world maintains itself in its integrity. Her role is to control the regularity of cosmic phenomena and to watch over the proper working of social rules. The deities feed upon her so as to be able to maintain the universal harmony she personifies. The offerings to ***Ma'at*** are one of the main acts of the daily divine cult: to forget them would be to risk a victory of the forces of chaos that threaten the world. She has to be respected so that the natural phenomena that guarantee life may come back.

When the heart is being weighed, ***Ma'at*** is placed on one of the two scales of the balance and has to determinate the weight of the faults of the deceased. No one can avoid this trial before reaching the kingdom of ***Osiris***; it allows the tribunal to ascertain whether the soul of the deceased was in conformity with the "principle of ***Ma'at***," that is to say, if it is in harmony with the moral rules of Egyptian society. In everyday life, she is the personification of all the notions related to justice and truth. The vizier, head of the executive power and the whole administration, is called "priest of ***Ma'at***," because he guarantees the moral order. His emblem is a small figurine of the goddess that he wears on his breast. In the same way, "to speak according to ***Ma'at***" is to tell the truth. ***Ma'at*** is, then, a compulsory deity since everyone, whether god, king or simple mortal, has to live according to her rule. As she is a goddess incarnating a universal principle, she had no specific temple. But she is present in all the sanctuaries of the Nile valley, especially in the scenes depicting daily rituals: they show the pharaoh offering a figurine of ***Ma'at*** to the god the temple is dedicated to. Whatever the document in which she appears, her iconography is always the same; she is depicted as a woman with an ostrich feather on her head, or simply just as an ostrich feather, which is the hieroglyph used to write her name.

# *Min*

Min 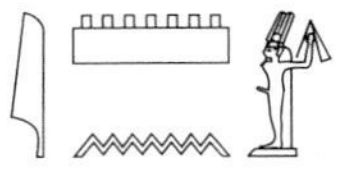

God of fertility; master of the routes of the oriental desert

Principal places of worship: Akhmin and Qift

Representation: a man with an erect penis, the right arm lifted up squarely behind his head and carrying a flail

His iconography may seem surprising at first, but this apparent immodesty is in direct relation with his function and has no perverse connotation. ***Min*** is simply a god of fertility and reproduction, as well as a generating principle. This is why he is depicted as a mummiform man with an erect penis, and why one uses the term ithyphallic to describe him. His right arm is lifted squarely behind his head, and by way of a scepter, he carries the flail, the royal insignia. His crown is the same as ***Amun***'s, the god of the Kingdom. His mummiform sleeve is part of a tradition in which all gods connected to the underground world, or to the vital and creative forces in the act of releasing themselves, are represented swaddled. Sometimes his flesh is blackened to recall a particular ritual that is practiced on certain feast days: to assert his fertilizing functions, the priest covers the statues of ***Min*** with a fortifying and stimulating substance that was made from charred coal mixed with bitumen. The festivities that are consecrated to him foretell the harvests, at the beginning of the season of **Chemu**. Salads, which later will be called romaines, were offered to him then, because their sap is supposed to have aphrodisiac qualities.

In **Coptos** and **Akhmin**, two towns situated north of **Thebes**, he is worshipped as the protector of the caravans leaving for the eastern desert. Roads leading to the Arabic desert and to the Middle Eastern countries leave from these towns. In the texts, ***Min***, *"the rich with perfume,"* is the *"master of the lapis-lazuli and malachite"* and is the *"master of the foreign nations of the East."* In this part of the country, his cult seems to go back to the most ancient times. In those days, he must certainly have received a cult in a sanctuary situated at the entrance of the mountain. Traces of this ancient devotion appear in certain specific documents: behind the image of ***Min*** is a chapel dug into a pointed rock.

## *Montu*

Montu 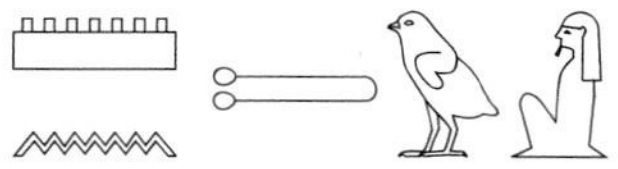

*Associated in a triad with the goddess Rattawy (the female sun) and the goddess infant Iunyt*

*A warrior god from the Theban area*

*Principal places of worship: Armant, Tod and Medamud (Upper Egypt)*

*Representation: a man wearing a falcon's head and the high double feathered crown*

This falcon god of Theban origin is the personification of the irresistible force of war. The texts explain that for this unusual deity *"who can make greater gods obey him,"* there is no earthly nourishment: *"hearts are his bread and blood is his water."* But for reasons connected with the different political choices of the realm, he had not always been very popular throughout Egyptian history.

Quite naturally, he does not appear very much in the Old Kingdom, since the pharaohs do not engage in big territorial conquests and there is no invasions threatening the country. In return, he becomes very popular from the Middle Kingdom onwards. At the end of the First Intermediate Period, under the 11th Dynasty, several kings claim a relationship with him, and add his name to their titles; thus *Mentuhotpe* simply means "***Montu*** is satisfied." After a long troubled period, a prince of **Thebes** unifies the country under a single sovereign and inaugurates the Middle Kingdom. The pharaohs of the 12th Dynasty, inheritating a unified country, decide to enlarge the boundaries of Egypt: they subdue **Nubia** and even campaign into Asian countries. They therefore build several temples in the honor of ***Montu***, the war god of the Kingdom. These places of worship are all in the Theban area, for ***Montu*** is essentially a Theban god.

In his most famous sanctuary, at **Tod**, he is associated in a triad with two feminine deities, the goddess ***Rattawy***, the female sun, and the child goddess ***Iunyt***. In 1936, an Asian treasure under the name of *Amenemhet II* was discovered. Many precious objects were found in four chests hidden in the sand: some rough and carved lapis-lazuli, objects in silver and gold, ingots of argentiferous lead or gold, amulets and seals, cylinders, cups and chains…

During the New Kingdom, the personality of ***Montu*** is gradually overtaken by the growing power of the god ***Amun*** of Thebes. He loses his universal characteristics which become those of the new state god, and his competency is limited to warfare. During the battles, he stands close to the pharaoh who likes to compare himself to this fierce and valiant god. The famous battle of **Qadesh** between *Ramesses II*, king of Egypt and *Muwattali,* king of the Hittites, is told in this fashion: *"His Majesty* (Ramesses II) *went by the fortress of Sile, as strong as Montu when he moves. All the countries tremble before him and their chiefs lay their tributes at his feet. All his opponents bow their heads fearing the authority of His Majesty."*

## *Mut*

Mut 

*Associated in a triad with the god Amun and with the god-son Khons*

*Goddess adored as consort of Amun*

*Principal places of worship: Karnak and Luxor (Upper Egypt)*

*Representation: a woman wearing the corpse of a vulture on her head*

Religious texts designate the goddess ***Mut*** by one hieroglyph which represents a vulture seen from the side. So why not give her the characteristics and personality of a vulture goddess as ***Nekhbet***, protector of Upper Egypt? For many years, when the deciphering of hieroglyphs was at its beginning, this was a rather common thesis. Nowadays, our knowledge of the Egyptian language allows us to give this hypothesis more nuance.

We know that the signs can have several and quite different values: they are used as **phonograms** (a sign used for one, two or three consonants or semi-consonants), **ideograms** (a sign symbolizing an idea and allowing a transcription of a word with just one sign) or **determinative** (a sign used to qualify the word preceding it). If some people have thought that the vulture of the goddess ***Mut*** had to be considered as an **ideogram**, today we are almost certain that it has to be interpreted as a simple **phonogram**, to be put in relation with the word *mwt*, which in hieroglyphic language means "the mother."

**Montu the warrior god**

*Montu is the warrior god of Egypt's New Kingdom, and during the battles, the pharaoh puts himself under his protection. However, as everything else connected to the New Kingdom, Montu is closely associated with Amun. Just as Min represents only the creative facet of Amun, Montu represents only the warrior aspect of the great dynastic god. This is why he wears the high double feathered crown, since Amun's personality is hidden behind Montu's. On this relief in the temple of Karnak, King Tuthmosis III is wearing the crown of Upper Egypt, and breathes in life through the ankh cross. Behind him is the falcon god, Montu, who has put his arm around his shoulders as a sign of protection.*

Temple of Karnak,
New Kingdom,
East Thebes, Upper Egypt.

This thesis is strengthened by the fact that in her iconography, there is no image of this goddess depicted in a purely zoomorphic fashion. Sometimes she wears the corpse of a vulture on her head, but this emblem is not reserved to her; many feminine deities, queen mothers and sovereigns wear this headdress as a crown. So it would be more legitimate to credit her with the qualities of a mother goddess, narrowly associated with the queens and queen mothers of Egypt.

When **Thebes** becomes the capital of the kingdom, ***Mut*** is an extremely popular deity, since she is the consort of ***Amun***, god of the Kingdom, and mother of ***Khons***, the child god of the Theban triad. She receives a special sanctuary in **Karnak**, where a great temple is dedicated to ***Amun***. Her domain, surrounded by a wall, is situated south of ***Amun***'s temple: they were connected by a large avenue, called a **dromos,** bordered on each side by sphinxes for 900 feet. Nowadays it is deteriorated, but archaeological excavations have brought to light another temple, built under the 18th Dynasty in the reign of *Amenhotep III*, in which some very interesting statues were found that reveal a special aspect of the goddess ***Mut***.

It seems that after the beginning of the New Kingdom, she took on the personality and aspect of lioness deities, called dangerous goddesses, such as ***Sakhmet***. In time, the characters of the two goddesses ended by complementing each other, then by merging, to result in an ambivalent deity, connected to ***Sakhmet*** for her destructive force and to ***Mut*** for her pacific aspect. Henceforth ***Mut*** assumes the qualities of a beneficent and healing goddess to palliate the destructions of the warrior goddess ***Sakhmet***. It is then in the honor of this double deity that ***Mut***'s sanctuary in **Karnak** was built. The Egyptians knew the tremendous possibilities of this goddess with many facets, and didn't hesitate to venerate her when they were hurt in any way. According to their beliefs, she was capable of sending all kinds of sufferings on earth, whether diseases, wars, famines or epidemics, so she was also able to stop them. *Amenhotep III*, who was said to have been struck by an incurable illness, did this: begging for his recovery, he offered ***Mut*** almost six hundred statues bearing the effigy of the lion goddess ***Sakhmet***. The most beautiful ones now belong to museums, but there are still a few lying in the ruins of the sanctuary.

**The lotus Nefertem**

*Nefertem symbolizes the primeval lotus from which the sun emerged at the beginning of time. So his emblem is naturally the lotus flower, preferably blue, which he wears on his head, as is shown here with this earthenware figurine. Nefertem is apparently walking; his chin is adorned with a fake beard and he wears a high and stylized lotus flower crown. This iconography of Nefertem is not unique: there can be differences. Sometimes the simple representation of the bloomed lotus flower is enough to evoke this deity. In the same way, the images showing a head coming out of a blossomed lotus flower refer to Nefertem and symbolize the sun god emerging from the original lotus.*

Late Period.

## *Nefertem*

Nefertem 

*Associated in a triad with the god Ptah and the goddess Sakhmet*

*God of the primeval lotus flower*

*Principal place of worship: Memphis (Lower Egypt)*

*Representation: a man wearing an open lotus flower*

***Nefertem*** is a deity born of the primeval lotus flower, and so he is represented by the blue lotus. Generally, he is depicted as a young man wearing an open lotus flower or a composite crown constituted of different elements: a lotus flower topped with two feathers and two collars acting as counterweights symbolizing fertility. A belief born in **Hermopolis** explains that the sun would be born of *"a great lotus that came out of the primeval waters."* Indeed, in this tradition, at the beginning of the world, a chalice of a closed lotus flower floats on the ***Nun***, the primeval ocean. A very strong beam of light will compel the lotus to stir and blossom. And from the opened petals the sun will burst out. In the evening, when it arrives to the west, the sun comes to find refuge in the lotus flower which then closes its petals. In the morning, the petals bloom and free the sun so that it would shine on the world with all its rays. This belief explains the close relationship between ***Re'*** and ***Nefertem***.

In the "**Pyramid Texts**," ***Nefertem*** is described as *"the lotus bud that is in front of the nose of **Re'**."* The episode tells the story of one of the numerous revolts fomented against ***Re'***. In this story, ***Re'*** is still a boy, but his enemies try to eliminate him, and decide to attack him at day break, when he was still in the east. Then follows a terrible fight *"in the sky as on earth,"* which ends in a victory for the partisans of ***Re'***. The plotters are then given to the sun god on the fiery island of **Shmoun**. A rather surprising detail tells us that at the time of the decisive battle, ***Re'*** carried a lotus flower to his nose, which was ***Nefertem***. Depending on the town where he is worshipped as a cult, ***Nefertem*** is associated with different deities. In **Memphis**, he is the son of ***Ptah*** and the goddess ***Sakhmet***. In the Nile Delta, in **Bubastis**, he is considered to be the son of the cat goddess ***Bastet***. Further north, in **Buto**, he is the son of the cobra goddess ***Wadjit***. Here he is the *"protector of the Two Lands"* and probably symbolizes the unification of Upper and Lower Egypt.

# *Neith*

Neith 

Associated with Khnum (in Esna) and mother of the crocrodile god Sobek

demiurge in the town of Esna

Places of worship: Sais (Lower Egypt), Esna (Upper Egypt)

Representation: a woman wearing the red crown of Lower Egypt or her emblem (two bows and a sheath)

***Neith*** is the goddess of the town of **Sais,** situated in the western Delta of the Nile. She is represented as a woman wearing the red crown of Lower Egypt, or her emblem: two bows tied together in their sheath. She is one of the rare goddesses in the Egyptian pantheon to be considered as a demiurge. In that function, she is androgynous: *"two thirds of her body are male, one third is female... The Two Countries are feasting, for their Mistress, god and goddess, shines above them."* Many texts explain this myth of creation: the ones that are the most complete are on the walls of the temple in **Esna**. Here ***Neith*** shares the role of demiurge with ***Khnum***, the potter god with the head of a ram.

She is considered to be *"the great primeval mother,"* who gives birth to the sun and the universe. At the beginning of time, she appears as a cow, ***Ihet***, floating on the ***Nun***: *"the Father of Fathers, the Mother of Mothers, the divine being who was the first to exist at the beginning was in the middle of the* ***Nun****; she came out of herself when the earth was still in the darkness and no plant grew. She took the aspect of a cow, that no deity anywhere could know."* Then, by simple evocation of their name, she formed thirty gods who have to help her in her creation: *"O You who have made us of whom we are the children, make us know what we don't know yet, for a look, the hill is barren, and we do not know what must come into existence."* After having thought for a long time about how the world and its elements should be made, the goddess ***Neith***, here as the cow ***Ihet***, explains to her progeny, the thirty primeval gods, that she will give birth to an exceptional deity, the sun: *"Today a sublime god will appear. When he opens his eye, the light will appear; when he closes it, the darkness will be back. Men will be born of the tears of his eye, and gods from the saliva of his lips. I shall make him strong with my strength, I shall make him bright with my brightness, I shall make him powerful with my power... For he is my son, come out of myself, and he shall be the king of this country for ever. I shall protect him and will carry him in my arms so that nothing can touch him. I will tell you his name: he shall be* ***Khepri*** *at dawn,* ***Atum*** *in the evening and he shall be the shining god for eternity in his name of* ***Re'*** *every day."*

Then the whole creation is organized in a totally logical fashion. One day, as ***Re'*** cannot find his mother, he starts to cry: *"the men came into existence through his tears."* After having found her, he started to salivate: *"the gods came to existence through his saliva."* Another day, unfortunately, it's ***Neith*** who spits in the ***Nun***. Disgusted, the gods repel the spittle: *"then it became a snake a hundred cubits long, who was called Apophis."* Later, ***Thoth*** appears: *"he came out of the heart of* ***Re'*** *in a moment of sadness."* Thus, all through the tale, all the elements of creation fit into place. Then ***Neith*** decides to go to **Sais**. She adopts her form as the cow ***Ihet*** and places the solar god between her horns to protect him against his enemies incarnated by the snake ***Apophis***. It is told that her trip lasted four months. One evening at last she arrives in **Sais**. ***Re'*** asks the divine assembly to organize a great feast in her honor, for the trip had been long and difficult: *"Welcome Neith today. Come for her and feast on this day of rejoicing, for she brought me here safe and sound. Light torches for her. Feast in her honor until daybreak."*

Besides her part as a demiurge, ***Neith*** has many functions that allow her to appear regularly in the legends and myths born in the different religious sites of the Nile Valley. She appears frequently as an archer goddess: with her bow and arrows, she repels the powers of evil and protects the hunters. She is also the patroness of the weavers, and because of the mysterious symbolism of weaving, she becomes the incarnation of rational science. Her name alone evokes wisdom and reason; she becomes the discerning counselor of the deities who like to ask her advice when they need help. She is also supposed to be the mother of the crocodile god ***Sobek***. Along with her terrestrial functions, she also has influence on the next world; with ***Isis***, ***Nephthys*** and ***Serket***, she watches over the deceased and his **canopic jars**, particularly the one that contains the stomach.

**The goddess Neith**

*She is a native of the town of Sais, where she is venerated as protector of the Delta of the Nile, but her influence spreads out much further. Her field of activity is vast: she acts as patroness of the weavers, as demiurge, as mistress of rational science, and as warrior goddess... She generally appears as a woman, wearing a long tight dress and the crown of Lower Egypt. On this stela that was found in Naucratis, a town south of Alexandria, the two scenes, perfectly symmetrical and identical, depict the goddess Neith sitting opposite Nectanebo I, first pharaoh of the 30th Dynasty. The text was written in the form of a decree, and stipulates that the clergy of Sais will be permitted to collect one tenth of all the foreign goods that come into town.*

Late Period.

## Nekhbet and Wadjit

*On the second terrace of Hatshepsut's funerary temple in Deir el-Bahri, there is a chapel consecrated to Anubis, the god of mummification. The main room is still very well preserved, especially the colors that have kept all their freshness. Along the top, the walls are decorated with images that depict the two guardian goddesses of the Kingdom and Horus, protector of the whole realm: the vulture Nekhbet of Upper Egypt, the cobra Wadjit from Lower Egypt and the falcon Horus of the "Two Lands". Here, we see the falcon with extended wings as it decorates a corner and, above it, a frieze of cobras Wadjit. They carry the chen sign, which is a circle of rope tied with a knot, that symbolizes the universe, or "what the sun encircles."*

Temple of Queen Hatshepsut
Deir el-Bahri,
New Kingdom.
West Thebes, Upper Egypt.

# *Nekhbet*

Nekhbet 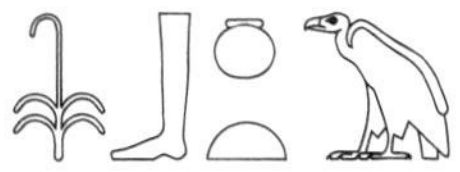

Goddess protector of the Upper Egypt

Principal place of worship: El-Kab (Upper Egypt)

Representation: a vulture wearing the white crown of the South

***Nekhbet***, "She of **Nekheb**," is the vulture goddess of the town of **Nekheb,** now called **El-Kab** in Upper Egypt. She is the guardian of Upper Egypt, just as ***Wadjit***, the cobra from **Buto**, represented the North country. Both of them were the protectors of the pharaoh, the "king of the Two Lands." Among the titles of the king, his second name recalls this double protection: it is the **Nebti name**, that is the **name of the two Ladies**. The cobra and the vulture are both settled on the sign *nb*, a basket. This hieroglyphic sign is the respectful name used to qualify the "lord," and by deduction, the king, god, or any person of quality. In the **Nebti name**, this association designates the pharaoh in relation with the two goddesses, guardians of Lower and Upper Egypt, and mainly shows that the whole country is under the rule of one authority. This is why the image of the two goddesses is everywhere in the royal iconography. Very often, ***Nekhbet*** is depicted as a vulture with widely spread wings. She wears the white crown of the south, sometimes with two high feathers, and holds in her claws the chen sign. This sign, in the form of a round cartouche, is a symbol for *"what the sun encircles during its course,"* that is the universe. Sometimes, she appears as a vulture at rest sitting next to the cobra ***Wadjit***, or encircling with ***Wadjit***, a name or a symbol charged with power. Both of them are depicted on pectorals or ornaments, here and there, with the solar god, a royal cartouche, an **wedjat** eye, a **djed** pillar...

Just as she watches over the pharaoh, the goddess ***Nekhbet*** also protects the queens of Egypt. The image of the vulture often appears in the composition of the crowns of the queens, and in their jewelry and adornments. She becomes in time the guardian of the oriental **wadi**. **Nekheb,** the town she comes from, is south of **Luxor**, on the eastern side of the Nile. She therefore controls all the roads that lead to the stone quarries of the **Wadi Hammamat**, or to the gold mines in the eastern desert.

## Duality in Egypt

| | | |
|---|---|---|
| *Region of Egypt* | South | North |
| *Name* | Upper Egypt | Lower Egypt |
| *Royal crown* | White Crown | Red Crown |
| *Protective Goddess* | Nekhbet | Wadjit |
| *Animal linked to the goddess* | Vulture | Cobra |
| *Residence of the Goddess* | El-Kab | Buto |
| *Protective god* | Seth | Horus |
| *Animal linked to the god* | Mythical animal | Falcon |
| *Heraldic plant* | Lotus | Papyrus |
| *Symbol* | Bee | Reed |

The cult of ***Nekhbet*** grows from 18th Dynasty on. The town of **Nekheb** then becomes the capital of the third nome district of Upper Egypt and the pharaohs give a sanctuary to the town that never ceases to grow until the Greco-Roman Period. Today there only remains the mud brick enclosure of the town; it is worthwhile to note because of its impressive size. Little by little, the personality of the vulture goddess grows richer: ***Nekhbet*** becomes the protector of births. This function probably comes from the part she plays as guardian of little ***Horus*** in the "**Legend of Osiris**." This episode tells how, after his birth, ***Horus*** has to live in hiding to escape from his uncle ***Seth***. To do this, ***Isis*** hides her son in the marshes of the Delta. She entrusts him to the care of her sister ***Nephthys*** and of the goddesses ***Wadjit*** and ***Nekhbet***; they become the wet nurses and the servants of the child. Because of this role as guardian of births, the Greeks merged ***Nekhbet*** with the goddess **Eileithya** (**Ilithye**) and renamed the town of **Nekheb**, **Eileithiyaspolis**.

*Previous pages*

**Nephthys and Isis, Anubis and Horus**

*These plates made of gold show four deities who play a very important part in the next world. On the first one, Isis and Nephthys are kneeling in front of an impressive djed pillar, symbol of duration and stability. Each deity wears her emblem on her head: the throne for Isis, and the plan of a house topped with a basket for Nephthys. On the other plate, Anubis and Horus are wearing the pschent, the crown of Lower and Upper Egypt. They are standing next to the magical knot, the girdle of Isis, symbol of protection. They are both identified with the linked animal: the jackal of Anubis and the hawk of Horus.*

Greco-Roman Period.

## *Nephthys*

Nephthys 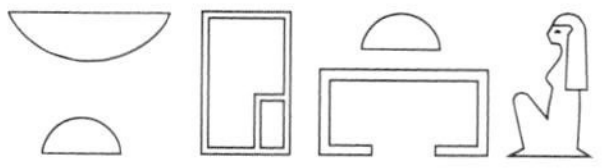

Daughter of Geb, the earth, and Nut, the sky

Sister of Isis, Osiris, Horus the Elder and Seth; wife of Seth

Protector of the deceased with her sister Isis

Representation: a woman wearing the two hieroglyphs of her name

The name of ***Nephthys*** rarely appears without her sister's, **Isis**. In fact the two of them give an image of inseparable deities who symbolize perfect sisterhood. They belong to the last divine generation of the Ennead of **Heliopolis**: they are daughters of ***Geb***, the earth, and ***Nut***, the sky, and they are the sisters of ***Osiris***, ***Seth***, and ***Horus the Elder***. The eldest daughter, ***Isis***, is united to ***Osiris*** and the younger one, ***Nephthys,*** married to ***Seth***. But these official unions do not in any way exclude a few infidelities. It is told for instance that the jackal ***Anubis*** is sired by ***Osiris,*** after an illegitimate union with ***Nephthys***. Whatever their function, the two sisters are complementary. Isis is the mother of ***Horus*** and ***Nephthys*** his wet nurse: *"He is **Horus**, his mother **Isis** brought him into the world and **Nephthys** raised him."* ***Isis*** is the wife of ***Osiris***, and ***Nephthys*** his lover. ***Isis*** symbolizes birth and light, whereas ***Nephthys*** is the incarnation of darkness and death. They are therefore impossible to separate. As opposed to ***Isis***, who is personally venerated in several towns of the country, ***Nephthys*** has no existence of her own. She generally appears with her sister on funerary occasions, watching over the body of the deceased. Her role as protector of the dead comes from the part she plays in the "**Legend of Osiris**," where she appears in all the episodes of the passion of ***Osiris***. She is particularly present in the very famous text that is chronologically situated just after ***Seth*** has dismembered the body of ***Osiris***. The two sisters then set off to search for all the pieces that have been strewn across Egypt, and mourn him in endless wailing. This splendid hymn is a long loving complaint that sings divine resurrection and rebirth to life: *"Thanks to us, you have forgotten sadness. We gather your limbs for you and look after your body. Come towards us then, that we might forget your enemy. Come then in the body you had on earth. Drive your anger away, and grant us your mercy, O Lord. Take back the heritage of the Double Land, O God unique whose projects are good for the deities... Come back without fear to your home..."*

So, in the next world, they look after the body of the deceased just as they looked, long ago, after ***Osiris***'s body. ***Isis*** stands at the foot of the coffins, and ***Nephthys*** at the head. She is depicted as a woman wearing a headdress made from the two hieroglyphs that are used to write her name: *neb,* the basket, and *hwt,* the plan of a house. Her name, ***Nebhwt***, turned by the Greek into ***Nephthys***, means "the Lady of the house." The two goddesses must help the deceased in his last voyage and insure his resurrection. With ***Serket*** and ***Neith***, they also protect the canopic jars, in which are preserved the viscera of the deceased.

## THE PROTECTION OF THE CANOPIC JARS OF THE DECEASED

| | | | |
|---|---|---|---|
| SOUTH | *ISIS*<br>Woman wearing the hieroglyphic signs of her name on her head (a throne) | *IMSET*<br>spirit with the head of a **man** | protection of the **liver** |
| NORTH | *NEPHTHYS*<br>Woman wearing the hieroglyphic signs of her name (basket and house plan) | *HAPY*<br>spirit with the head of a **baboon** | protection of the **lungs** |
| EAST | *NEITH*<br>Woman wearing an emblem representing two bows linked together in their sheath | *DUAMUTEF*<br>spirit with the head of a **jackal** | protection of the **stomach** |
| WEST | *SERKET*<br>Woman wearing a scorpion or a headless grub on her head | *QEBEHSENUF*<br>spirit with the head of a **falcon** | protection of the **intestines** |

# *Nun*

Nun 

**Primeval watery abyss representing emptiness and preceding creation in different cosmogonies, especially in Heliopolis, Hermopolis and Memphis**

*"Before the existence of the sky, before the existence of the earth, before the existence of men, and before the existence of death,"* was ***Nun***. This excerpt of the "**Coffin Texts**" sums up the nature of the first element. The term ***Nun*** could actually be translated as non-being, nothingness, what exists before anything and that doesn't exist, for which reason ***Nun*** is indefinable. So to describe it, the Egyptians chose to explain what the contributions of creation are; by deduction, ***Nun*** must be understood as the opposite of the created world. It is most likely a watery immensity of inert waters, a disorganized chaos, an unlimited amount of space that is steeped in total and absolute darkness. It is supposed to contain all the possibilities of being, to screen the intimate substance of things, and to possess all the faculties: the stimulation of this tremendous potentiality must permit the act of creation.

*"I was alone with **Nun**, in inertia, and I could not find a place to stand up; I could not find a place to sit down. The town of **Heliopolis** where I was to live had not yet been founded; the throne upon which I was to sit had not yet been made... The gods of the first generation had not yet come into existence, the Ennead of primeval gods did not exist, for they were still within me..."*

The "**Coffin Texts**" tell us that ***Nun*** shelters a force that is materialized by an unconscious and inert being: the demiurge. This term designates the creative god, who for no particular reason one day will feel life kindle within himself. In the beginning, ***Nun*** has no consciousness of this awakening: it doesn't realize that the demiurge is stirring into existence. Necessarily, this transformation must drive the creative god to dissociate himself from ***Nun*** to become a creature in his own right. His first act will be to model a body for himself, since the demiurge is his own creator as the texts say, *"he came to existence from himself,"* with neither father nor mother. In the same way, he forms a few snakes to help him in his task: these hybrid and deformed beings help the demiurge, but do not belong to the organized world, since once the creation is finished, they are condemned to disappear.

But a question remains: what happens to ***Nun*** once the world is created? Against all expectations, ***Nun*** remains after the creation. But it is pushed back to the rims of the world, and it surrounds the universe. In *the Inquiry*, **Herodotus** gives an account of a belief concerning the sources of the Nile: *"The second theory is less erudite but it is filled with more marvel: the Nile undergoes this phenomenon (the floods) because it is born from the Ocean that surrounds the whole earth with its waters."* But he quickly adds: *"I do not know for myself of any river Ocean; I expect Homer or some other ancient poet may have invented this name for one of his fables."* This "Ocean" mentioned by **Herodotus** is none other than ***Nun***. It is also told that the sun falls into ***Nun*** every evening before reappearing every morning. But very often, this space steeped in darkness is considered to be an inhospitable immensity that shelters threatening forces and maleficent creatures that never cease to agitate it. Nun is also the place where ***Apophis***, the gigantic snake who tries to overturn the sun boat, lives. It is also in ***Nun*** that the poor souls that have not been able to reach the kingdom of ***Osiris*** wander. All these forces never cease to threaten the equilibrium of the creation, and constantly express the resurgent requirement of chaos: to win back the organized world. We have to acknowledge that often the texts evoke the eventual victory of ***Nun***, which would lead inevitably to the end of the world.

*"The plains will be dammed up, the two extremities of the world will be brought together and the banks will meet, the travelers will be unable to use the roads, the slopes will be destroyed for those who want to leave..."* A day shall come, when the gods, creatures and deceased will have spent their time, when the world will cease to exist. But this end is not the absolute end, because what has not been created cannot be destroyed: on that day, ***Nun*** and the demiurge, before the creation, will find each other and will become one single being. They will take possession of the whole space; the demiurge will loose all consciousness and will plunge back, inert, into the primeval ocean... until a new cycle of creation comes to disrupt the chaos.

# Nut

> Nut 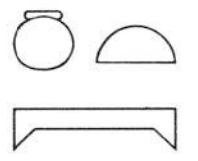
>
> *Daughter of Shu, vital breath, and Tefnut, heat.*
>
> *Sister and wife of Geb*
>
> *Mother of Osiris, Horus the Elder, Isis, Seth and Nephthys*
>
> *Goddess who personifies the sky*
>
> *Representation: a woman forming the heavenly vault with her starry body, or as a huge celestial cow*

***Nut*** comes from the cosmogony of **Heliopolis**, in which she is the goddess of the sky and is coupled with her brother and husband ***Geb***, the earth. She is generally depicted in the reliefs as a woman bent over the earth, her head lying to the west and her feet standing in the east. But in other pictures, ***Nut*** is an immense heavenly cow rising above the earth. ***Nut*** symbolizes the space in which the sun travels. It makes two trips a day: the first one on the day body of ***Nut***, and the second on her night body. During the day, ***Re'*** travels along the stomach of the goddess, and lightens the world with his rays. In the evening, she swallows him to give birth to him in the morning again, victorious and rejuvenated; in the sky, the stars replace the sun.

There are many representations of the day and night trips of the sun that have been found in the Egyptian monuments, especially in the tombs of the **Valley of the Kings**. One of the most remarkable decorates the ceiling of the tomb of *Ramesses VI*. Two bodies inordinately long are back to back; they represent the diurnal and nocturnal bodies of the goddess. On the diurnal body of ***Nut***, twelve red discs probably represent the twelve hours of the day. Between the celestial vault and the earth flows a river upon which float the barks that symbolize the different hours of the day. The source of this river is situated close to the pubis of the goddess, at exactly the place that the two sun boats, diurnal and nocturnal, meet: it is here that every morning, ***Re'*** goes from one to another. On both riverbanks, spirits, mythical figures, deities, rowers and haulers watch and acclaim the passing of the sun boat and its crew. The day trip is full of traps and struggles against the cosmic enemy, the snake ***Apophis***, and it finishes close to the mouth of ***Nut***, into which ***Re'*** disappears to enter on his second journey.

The nocturnal body of ***Nut*** is recognizable by the stars that are strewn on it. This space is also divided into twelve hours, but the river has been replaced by a bed of sand upon which the boat floats. Each hour of the night is marked by a door that has to be passed. The trip seems to be very dangerous, for there is a multitude of small deities and spirits that surround the sun boat and its crew with torches, knives and lances, to protect it against the hostile forces, maleficent powers and evil spirits. At last, at the twelfth hour of the night, the bark arrives close to the thighs of the goddess. The sun can be reborn again and start on his diurnal voyage.

But for all her qualities of celestial goddess, one should not forget that ***Nut*** belongs to the cosmogony of **Heliopolis**. She is the daughter of ***Shu*** and ***Tefnut***, the wife of ***Geb***, and above all, the mother of five divine children whose births are rather unusual. The separation of the sky and the earth by ***Shu*** inevitably entails a fragmentation of time, which is punctuated by the course of the sun.

The solar year of three hundred and sixty days, is divided into twelve months of thirty days, each one of which has twenty-four hours. This separation was ordered by the demiurge, who was displeased to know that his grandchildren were secretly having amorous relations. He therefore forbade ***Nut*** to give birth during the periods included in the official calendar. But as the poor woman is expecting quintuplets, she sends for the god ***Thoth***, the master of time, who is said to be secretly in love with her. To save her from this predicament, he finds no other solution than to play dice with the moon: he wins the game and manages to secure five more days on the calendar. Thus ***Nut*** can bring her five children into the world: ***Osiris***, ***Horus the Elder*** (***Haroeris***), ***Seth***, ***Isis*** and ***Nephthys***.

Their peculiar birth, out of the standards of time, makes the divine community consider them as intruders. They soon acquire a very bad reputation: they are called the "children of disorder," and their unceasing quarrels cause time to be troubled. On the calendar, these five days correspond to the last five days of the year: they are called the additional days, or epagomenal days, as they are not included in the twelve months of the official calendar. They are an important transition between the end of year and the beginning of the next.

**Nut, the heavenly vault**

*On this stela of painted wood, the Lady Taperet presents herself in front of the god Atum. If his name had not been written above his head, he would be difficult to recognize, for nothing in his iconography allows his identification. Only two details show that he is really a god: the cross of life and the was scepter that he carries in his hands, which are two insignia that are generally kept for the gods. Above the scene, following the curve of the stela, the body of Nut bridges the sky. As goddess of the sky, stars and celestial lights form her garb. It is also along her body that the sun boat sails. The three suns here depict Re'-Atum-Khepri, the divinity with three facets. Close to her mouth is Atum, the setting sun; in the middle of her body is Re', the sun in all its glory; and close to her pubis is Khepri, the sun at daybreak.*

Third Intermediate Period.

# Osiris

Osiris 

*Son of Geb, the earth and Nut, the sky*
*Husband and brother of Isis*
*Principal place of worship: Abydos (Central Egypt)*
*Representation: a mummified man, wearing the atef crown, and holding the crook and the flail across his chest*

***Osiris*** is probably the most popular deity in the Egyptian pantheon. Of course his immense reputation is due to his function, because it concerns every mortal, whether kings or commoners: he is the god of the next world, and the god who guarantees all human resurrection. One can ignore him, since when the time comes, everyone yearns to join him in his kingdom.

However, ***Osiris*** was not always so popular: his personality is the fruit of a long evolution during which he will assimilate many divinities. In the beginning, he seems to incarnate the powers connected to the underground world and to fertility. Later, he integrates the cosmogony of **Heliopolis**. He becomes one of the sons of ***Geb*** and ***Nut***, and above all, ***Geb***'s heir apparent to the earthly throne. In **Memphis**, he assumes the funerary characters of ***Sokaris***, and in **Abydos**, he absorbs the personality of ***Khentimentiu***, god of the deceased and patron of the necropolis. Towards the end of the Old Kingdom, ***Osiris*** is the indisputable master of the underground world; in the next world, the deceased king becomes an ***Osiris***, a personality that will be adopted by all the deceased after the 12th Dynasty. Apart from that, he also has a celestial character inherited from ancient myths: he is **Orion**, one of the stars that shines at night, and he is also the moon or one of the aspects of the nocturnal sun when it travels through the underground world.

Of course, because of the very complex personality of ***Osiris***, the theologians will try to conceive a legend aimed at synthesizing the different aspects of the god. It is this tale that is currently called the "**Legend of Osiris**." No Egyptian document fully relates this beautiful legend; but here and there parts of texts describe passages of it. The complete tale actually comes from a work called *De Iside a Osiride*, written by the Greek author **Plutarch**. The "**Legend of Osiris**" is divided into three big chapters: the murder of ***Osiris***, the birth and childhood of ***Horus***, the battle between ***Horus*** and ***Seth*** for the earthly kingdom. These events seem to be clearly at the heart of divine preoccupations, for gods who do not seem to have any connection with the problem never cease to intervene. These quarrels have all kinds of repercussions, and the protagonists are engaged in complex struggles for power and unceasing fights.

***Osiris*** is the oldest child of ***Geb*** and ***Nut***, and is heir to his father's earthly kingdom. As a civilizing king, he teachs agriculture to men and tore the Egyptians *"away from their existence of privation and wild animals."* He also gives them their laws, teachs them how to respect the gods and brings them civilization. In this role, ***Osiris*** appears under the name of ***Wennefer***, the *"always good one."* Of course, ***Seth***, his brother, becomes jealous of him and plans to kill him. So he invites ***Osiris*** to a banquet with forty two other guests, who are his accomplices. During the feast, ***Seth*** brings a chest the size of ***Osiris***. The guests marvel at it and ***Seth*** promises to give it as a present to whoever could fill it perfectly by lying down in it. They all try in vain; ***Osiris*** tries and fills it perfectly. The guests immediately jump on to it to close it, lock it and throw it in the Nile. ***Isis*** then leaves to find her husband; she finally finds him in the port of **Byblos**. She comes back to Egypt with the body of ***Osiris***, and hides it in the Delta of the Nile. There she manages to conceive from her dead husband the little ***Horus***, who is born and brought up in the greatest secrecy. But ***Seth*** is informed by his accomplices of these events. He goes to the Delta and discovers the dead body of ***Osiris***; he cuts him into pieces that he scatters across Egypt. ***Isis***, with the help of her sister, ***Nephthys***, goes once more to look for him. She finds all the pieces except for the phallus that is said to have fallen into the river and to have been swallowed by an oxyrhinchus (a fish symbolizing ***Seth***). ***Isis*** and ***Anubis*** reconstitute ***Osiris***, and wrap his body with bandages, thus creating the first mummy. ***Thoth*** brings him back to life, but in a new form of existence, since from then on, ***Osiris*** reigns in the next world. Of course this myth must be understood as a sort of passion play. ***Osiris*** is a being who on earth is victim of a traitor and is put to death. But thanks to the solicitude and love of ***Isis,*** he overcomes this trial by being resuscitated. For this reason, everyone wants to identify with him in the next world, for he is the only one who brings to human beings the hope of eternal life.

**Osiris, god of the dead**

*This funerary papyrus offers a rather unusual image of Osiris. It is in fact the colors used by the artist that give this impression of originality: they are not common, dark and with little variety. But the end effect is superb, and is different from the classic image of the great god of the dead. Osiris is sitting under a dais, holding in his hands the flail, the was scepter with the head of a dog, and the heka crook. He wears the atef crown with two sideways high feathers and wears on his forehead two ram horns and an ureaus. On his mummified form appear the symbols of life (the ankh cross), of stability (the djed pillar) and of the divine (the was scepter). Close to him stands Nekhbet, the vulture goddess, protector of Upper Egypt, wearing the white crown of the south.*

New Kingdom.

**Tutankhamun protected by Nekhbet and Wadjit**

*In the treasure of Tutankhamun are many pieces of gold craftsmanship, especially the coffins and the funerary mask, which present the young king with a false beard and wearing the nemes. On his forehead are the emblems of Lower and Upper Egypt: the cobra Wadjit of the north and the vulture Nekhbet of the south. The two goddesses, represented side by side, symbolize the "Two Lands," Upper Egypt and Lower Egypt, and confirm the power and authority of the king over the whole territory.*

New Kingdom,
Egyptian Museum of Cairo.

## *Wadjit*

Wadjit 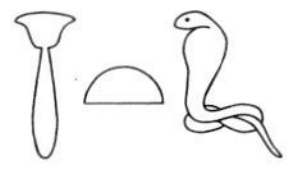

Goddess protector of Lower Egypt

Principal place of worship: Buto (Lower Egypt)

Representation: a cobra with its hood extended

***Wadjit***, "the Colored Papyrus" is the cobra goddess of **Per-Wadjit**, the "House of **Wadjit**." This town situated in Lower Egypt in the western part of the Delta of the Nile, is called today **Buto**, or in Arab, **Tell El Fara'in**, the "village of the Pharaohs."

Just as ***Nekhbet*** is the protector of Upper Egypt, ***Wadjit*** is the goddess of Lower Egypt and the Delta of the Nile. Represented together side by side, ***Nekhbet*** as a vulture and ***Wadjit*** as a cobra, they symbolize the kingdom at peace and assert the power of the king on "the Two Lands", Upper and Lower Egypt. ***Wadjit***'s iconography is always the same: she is depicted as a raised cobra wearing rather often the red crown of Lower Egypt.

The Royal Titulary is the expression used to designate the titles chosen by the pharaoh when he ascends to the throne of Egypt. It qualifies a sovereign by announcing his political program; it also has to distinguish him from his predecessors or successors. In the beginning, the kings have just one name: **the Horus name**. As early as the first dynasties, this protocol is enlarged and soon becomes a titulary of five names which recalls the characteristics and essential qualities of the Pharaoh. The goddesses ***Nekhbet*** and ***Wadjit*** are present in the second name of the king, the **Nebti name** or **He of the Two Ladies**, as warrants of the two kingdoms of Egypt: they must both ensure stability, union and peace to the land.

# ROYAL TITULARY

### NAME I - THE HORUS NAME

The king is presented as the incarnation of the falcon god ***Horus***. It is usually written in a **serekh**, stylized from a palace facade, topped with a falcon wearing the **pschent**. This royal headdress is a combination of the white crown of Upper Egypt and the red crown of Lower Egypt.

### NAME II - THE NEBTI NAME

The sovereign is put under the protection of the two guardian goddesses of Egypt: ***Nekhbet*** and ***Wadjit.*** The vulture ***Nekhbet*** of **El-Kab**, wearing the white crown of the South, is next to ***Wadjit*** of **Buto,** wearing the red crown of the North. The two goddesses each sit on a basket that represents the lord in hieroglyphic writing.

### NAME III - THE GOLDEN HORUS NAME

It confirms the divine and unfailing character of the body of ***Horus***, and in a wider sense, the body of the Pharaoh, who is the living incarnation of the god. It is introduced by the representation of a falcon sitting on the sign of gold, **nub**.

### NAME IV. THE THRONE NAME

It is the king's "first name" and proclaims his sovereignty over the two kingdoms of Egypt. It can also be translated as *"the one who belongs to the reed and to the bee."* This name is always set in a cartouche, a kind of oblong buckle that symbolizes the universal reign of the Pharaoh and ratifies his omnipotence over the world.

### NAME V - THE BIRTH NAME

It confers on the king solar filiation, and gives him a divine ascendancy. It is also inscribed in a cartouche, and it is the name that we generally use to name the pharaohs: *Khufu, Senusret, Amenhotep, Tuthmosis, Tutankhamun, Sethos, Ramesses...*

Here is for instance the titulary of *Ramesses II*:

**Name I** - *"Powerful bull loved by **Ma'at**"*
**Name II** - *"Protect Egypt, subdue the foreign countries"*
**Name III** - *"Rich in years, great in victories"*
**Name IV** - *"Strong in truth of **Re'**, chosen by **Re'**"*
**Name V** - *"**Re'** gave him birth, **Amun**'s loved one"*

# Ptah

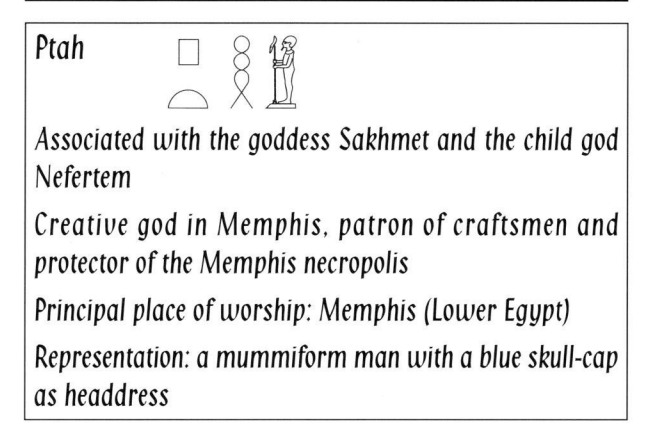

| Ptah 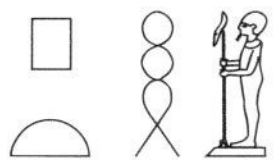 |
|---|
| Associated with the goddess Sakhmet and the child god Nefertem |
| Creative god in Memphis, patron of craftsmen and protector of the Memphis necropolis |
| Principal place of worship: Memphis (Lower Egypt) |
| Representation: a mummiform man with a blue skull-cap as headdress |

A native from **Memphis**, ***Ptah*** is one of the most important and prestigious gods of the Egyptian pantheon. He is depicted as a man wearing tight mummy wrappings, with only his arms free, holding a composite scepter made of three symbols that describe his personality: the **djed** pillar, which represents duration and stability; the **was** scepter, divinity; and the **ankh** cross, life. By way of hair or wig, he wears a small blue skull-cap.

In the beginning, the god ***Ptah*** is simply the patron of craftsmen, goldsmiths and sculptors. He is considered to be the creator of techniques and the arts, which is why he becomes the patron of craftsmen. With time, he absorbs the personality of ***Sokaris***, the funerary god of **Memphis** and protector of the necropolis, and then the personality of ***Osiris***: so under the name of ***Ptah-Sokar-Osiris***, he is venerated as the funerary god of the entire necropolis of **Memphis**. At the same time, he is related to the ***Apis*** bull, who is his official representative and his embodiment on earth. According to the narratives of **Herodotus**, the sacred bull would be born of a cow impregnated by ***Ptah***, who would manifest himself as a flash of lightning. Under the name of ***Ptah-Tanen***, he assimilates the god ***Tanen***, *"the earth that rises up"*; he thus becomes the incarnation of the depths of the earth and of the fertile ground from which all life comes. Because of his immense popularity, the **Memphis** clergy decides to give him a divine family and associates him in triad with ***Sakhmet***, the lioness deity, and ***Nefertem***, the lotus god.

However, apart from all the qualities that he acquires during the ages, ***Ptah*** is essentially a creative god. There is unfortunately only one rather late document still in existence, that speaks about the cosmogony of **Memphis**; it is a slab of granite from the 25th Dynasty, engraved under the reign of *Shabaqo* and found in ***Ptah***'s main sanctuary in **Memphis**. It indicates at the beginning that it is a copy of an older and very damaged papyrus, preserved in the records of the sanctuary: *"This text has been consecrated once more by His Majesty in the sanctuary of his father «**Ptah** south of his wall». His Majesty discovered that it was a very old piece of work, so worm-ridden that one could not understand it from beginning to end. After copying it, His Majesty has consecrated it once more in an even better state that it had been before... Thus did the son of **Re'**, Shabaqo, for his father **Ptah-Tanen**."* The original text most likely dates back to the end of the Old Kingdom, and has completely disappeared now. The version of the 25th Dynasty, probably changed and adjusted by the priests of the temple of ***Ptah***, has several blanks, since the stela was used afterwards as a millstone in the Arab and modern periods. So it is impossible for us to reconstitute for the moment the different elements of this creation.

This tradition is doubtless the most "intellectual" one that was ever elaborated by the Egyptian clergy, and it combines elements of **Heliopolis** and **Hermopolis**, but it gives to ***Ptah*** the role of creator: he is *"the one who engendered himself and who gave birth to the divine Ennead... He brought the gods to life. He founded the towns and nomes. He put the gods in their sanctuaries. He made their offerings plentiful and founded their chapels. He molded their bodies according to the wishes of their hearts."* He creates through the simple action of his spirit which projects the object to be created and with his tongue by uttering the idea, gives life to the different elements of the organized world: *"**Ptah** created sight thanks to the eyes, hearing thanks to the ears, and breathing thanks to the nose. They inform the heart. It is he who allows all knowledge to appear and it is the tongue that repeats what the heart has thought... For all divine words come out according to what the heart has conceived and what the tongue has ordered."* The simple act of pronouncing what has been imagined by the heart, center of thought, allows them to exist: *"Thus were created all labor and all art, the activity of hands, the use of feet, the movement of limbs, according to the order conceived by the heart and expressed by the tongue."* Which means that things only exist if they have a name. And indeed, it seems that for human beings, the name is a second creation; to name someone will make him exist, even beyond death.

**The god Ptah**

*Very often the deities adopt different representations, each image depending on which aspect of their personality is to be underlined. The iconographies also evolve as time elapses, as the gods acquire new personalities or when they are submitted to foreign influences. This is not the case for Ptah: whether creative god, protector of the necropolis in Memphis or patron of the craftsmen, whether in the Old Kingdom or in the Late Period, he always appears in the same guise. He stands up straight, his body sheathed in mummy wrappings, which is an attire reserved for deities related to fertility or to the next world. He does not wear a wig or a crown, but a skull cap, which is blue if the statue is colored. He holds in his hands the was scepter with the canine head which symbolizes divinity. Sometimes he also carries the djed pillar, symbol of duration and stability, and the ankh cross, symbol of life.*

Late Period.

# The weighing of the heart of Nesmin

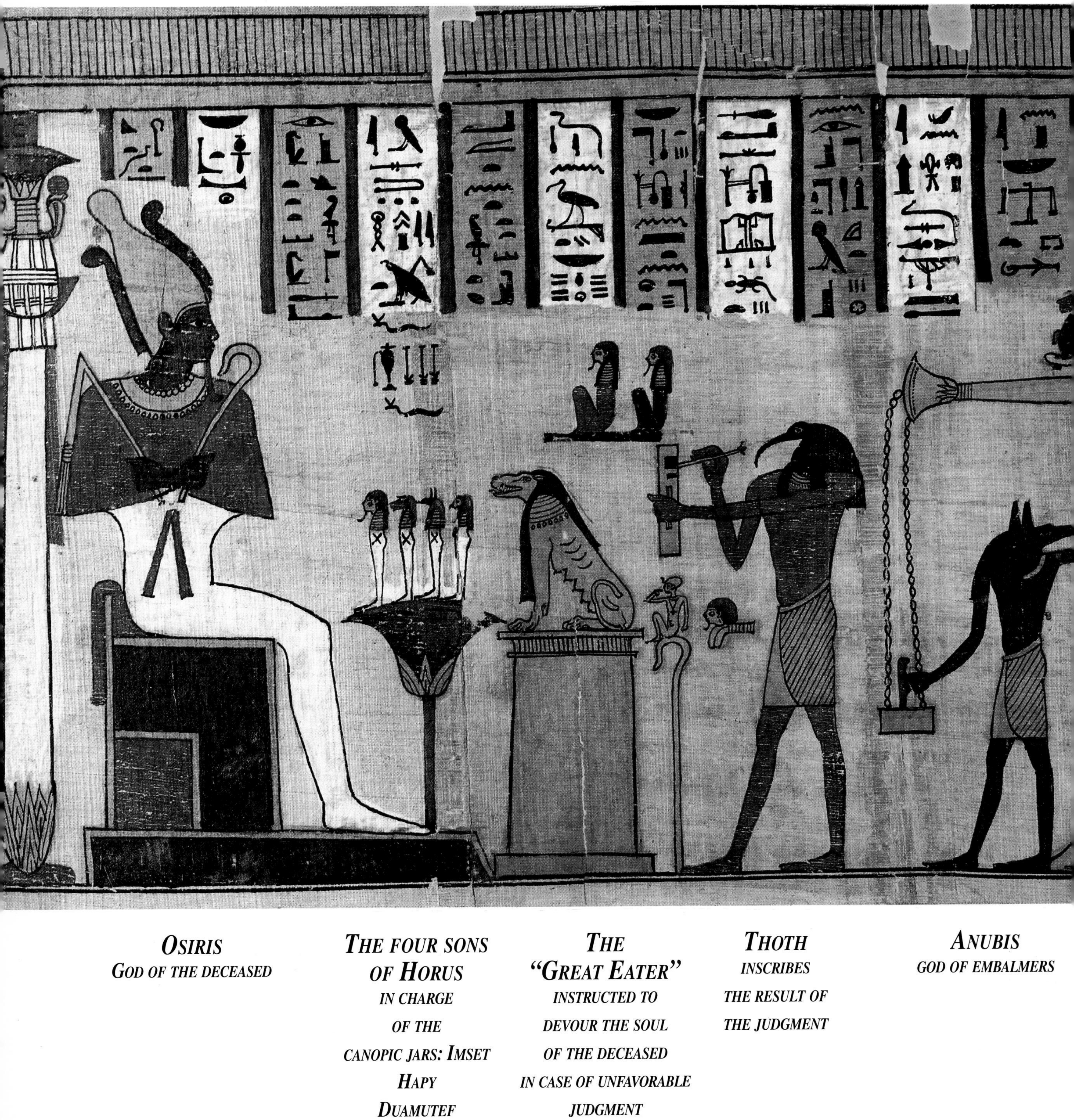

**Osiris**
God of the deceased

**The four sons of Horus**
in charge of the canopic jars: Imset, Hapy, Duamutef, Qebehsenuf

**The "Great Eater"**
instructed to devour the soul of the deceased in case of unfavorable judgment

**Thoth**
inscribes the result of the judgment

**Anubis**
God of embalmers

# PAPYRUS FROM THE LATE PERIOD (30TH DYNASTY)

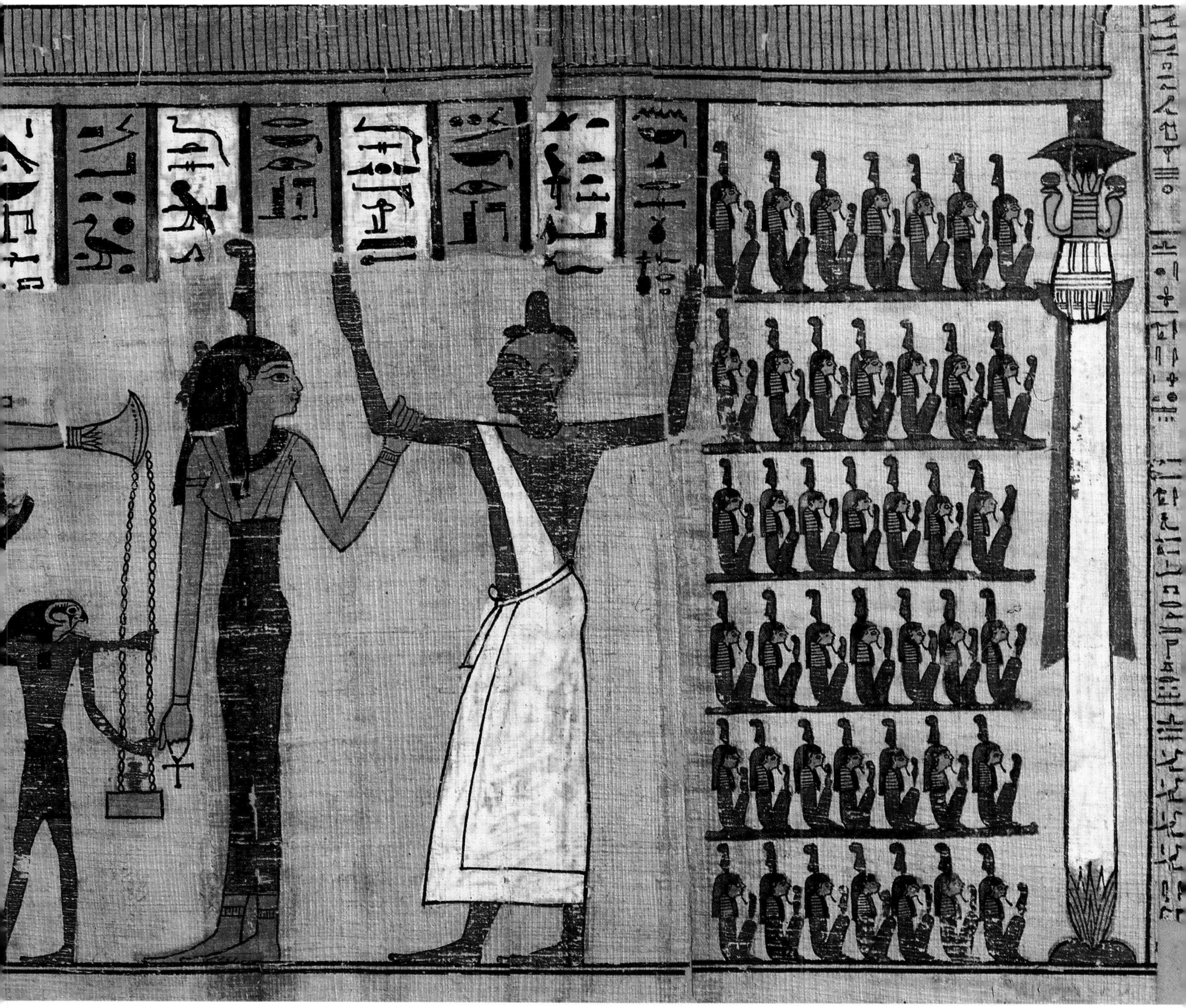

**HORUS**
CONTROLS THE
WEIGHING WITH ANUBIS

**THE DECEASED AND MA'AT**
GODDESS OF TRUTH AND JUSTICE

**THE FORTY-TWO DEITIES
OF THE JUDGMENT HALLS**
ASSIST OSIRIS
IN THE JUDGMENT OF THE DECEASED

## Four sons of Horus

**Spirit protectors of the canopic jars**

Qebehsenuf, spirit of the West

Ha' Py, spirit of the North

Duamutef, spirit of the East

Imset, spirit of the South

The Egyptians thought that every human being is constituted of different elements, some material and some spiritual. The spiritual principles comprise the energy, the spiritual body, an invisible power, and above all, the **ba** and the **ka**. The **ba**, which is more or less the soul, represents the spiritual part of the person that leaves the body when death comes and regains its own individuality to wander according to its will. Represented as a bird, the **ba** can either stay in the tomb, go into the funerary chamber, or go outside for a stroll on the favorite walks of the deceased. The **ka** is more difficult to describe, for there is no similar notion in our language. It is a manifestation of vital energies, conservative as well as creative, surviving all physical death. As for the material elements, they are the body, the heart and the name. The name exists as the second creation of the person: to mention the name of a person is to give him life beyond the physical disappearance of the body, which is why there are many inscriptions of the name of the deceased in his tomb and in his funerary temple.

The Egyptians thought that death is not an end, but a passage to another form of existence. Inevitably, this passage is very dangerous, because when death comes, the different elements of the human personality are scattered, each preserving its own integrity. If they can be all assembled once more, a second life is possible. So it is important to try to save what is most fragile, that is to say the body. To let it deteriorate is to lose all chance of survival, which is why mummification was invented. These operations are known thanks to **Herodotus**: *"First, with an iron hook, they extract the brain through the nostrils. But they only take out a small part of it; the rest they dissolve with certain drugs. Then, with a sharp stone from Ethiopia, they make an incision along the side of the abdomen and empty the body of its viscera."*

The bowels of the deceased are simply thrown away. Only four items are subject to a special treatment: they are mummified and placed into four urns called **canopic jars**. The viscera are put under the protection of four funerary goddesses and the ***four sons of Horus***. These spirits, who are supposed to be sons of the falcon god, take care of the liver, lungs, stomach and intestines during the lifetime. So, it seems perfectly logical that it should be they who take care of them in the next life.

At the same time, the ***four sons of Horus*** are called "Masters of the cardinal points," a function they keep as protectors of the **canopic jars**; each organ has to be properly oriented according to its tutelary god. Thus the rules that dictate the disposition of the canopic jars are very precise: ***Imset***, spirit of the South with the head of a man, watches with ***Isis*** over the liver; ***Hapy,*** spirit of the North with the head of a baboon, watches with ***Nephthys*** over the lungs; ***Duamutef,*** spirit of the East with the head of a jackal, watches with ***Neith*** over the stomach; ***Qebehsenuf,*** spirit of the West with the head of a falcon, watched with ***Serket*** over the intestines.

Once the organs have been removed from the body, **Herodotus** explains that: *"Once the cavity has been emptied, they cleanse it with palm wine and pulverized aromatic substances, they fill the belly with pure crushed myrrh, cinnamon and other aromatic substances, except for incense; then they sew up the body."* There are only the skin, bones and cartilage left that have to be dehydrated to avoid the decaying process. *"They saturate the body with salt by putting it in a bath of natron for seventy days; it shall not last any longer. Once the seventy days are up, they wash the body, and wrap it entirely with strips of fine linen coated with this gum that Egyptians use instead of glue."*

The mummification can require several hundred yards of linen, each limb being wrapped individually first, before wrapping the whole body afterwards. Before wrapping the body, the priest places on the opening that has been made in the body to take out the viscera, a small plate generally made out of precious metal for high ranking people; it is the "plate of evisceration" upon which the ***four sons of Horus*** are engraved, as a sign of protection and conservation.

*Earlier pages*

**The four sons of Horus**

*At the end of his trip through the infernal regions of the Underworld, the deceased enters in the judgment hall where the divine court is held, with Osiris sitting on the left of the scene, and the forty-two judges on the right. The most important part of the judgment is the weighing of the heart: Ma'at, goddess of justice and truth, and represented by an ostrich feather, is balanced with the heart of the deceased. The jackal Anubis, and the falcon Horus check the weighing, while Thoth, the divine scribe, waits to write down the verdict. If the judgment is favorable, that is, if the heart exactly balances Ma'at, the deceased is admitted to the kingdom of Osiris and will be able to enjoy eternal bliss in a second life. In the other case, he is thrown to a hybrid being, the "Great Eater," who gobbles him up, and he is condemned to wander forever in the chaos of the Nun. Sitting on a pedestal, the beast patiently waits for the verdict to be pronounced by Osiris. In front of it are the four sons of Horus, who watch over the viscera of the deceased in the next world: Imset, with the head of a man; Hapy, with the head of a baboon; Duamutef, with the head of a jackal; and Qebehsenuf, with the head of a falcon.*

Late Period.

# Re'

Re'

*Creative god in Heliopolis, who incarnates the sun at its zenith*

*Combined with many deities: Re'-Atum, Amun-Re', Re'-Harakhty, Sobek-Re', Khnum-Re'...*

*Principal place of worship: Heliopolis (Lower Egypt)*

*Representation: a man, sometimes with the head of a falcon, wearing the solar disc on his head*

***Re'*** is the main solar god of Egypt and he is venerated under this name in **Heliopolis.** There, he is the creative god and presides over the "Great Ennead," constituted of nine fundamental gods: ***Shu*** and ***Tefenet***, ***Geb*** and ***Nut***, ***Osiris***, ***Horus the Elder***, ***Isis***, ***Seth*** and ***Nephthys***. His role in the Egyptian pantheon is so important that, as early as the reign of *Khephren* in the 4th Dynasty, the pharaohs add a fifth name to their royal titulary: the **Birth name** (or **Son of Re'**). As the centuries go by, and the religions shift slowly, he is associated with many divinities who need solar help to develop their cult. This is especially true of the gods ***Amun***, ***Sobek*** or ***Khnum***, who become ***Amun-Re'***, ***Sobek-Re'*** or ***Khnum-Re'***.

Many myths describe ***Re'*** and his daily trips across the sky. At dawn, he rises in the east and gets into his "day boat" with his retinue. He travels through the twelve hours of the day and arrives in the west in the evening. There, he changes boats, gets into his "night boat" and travels through the night, which is equally divided into twelve hours. During this journey, when the earth is steeped in darkness, he illuminates the obscure regions of the other world. Afterwards, he reappears at dawn to start a new cycle again. During his diurnal trip, he adopts different names and guises: he is the beetle ***Khepri*** at dawn, the solar disc ***Re'*** at midday, and the aged man ***Atum*** at dusk.

***Re'*** also appears in all the legends which speak about his stay on earth when he was king of the gods and men, about his old age, and his departure for heaven. The "**Book of the celestial Cow**" tells in detail about the last years of his reign on earth and his departure to the sky. It is reproduced and illustrated in several crypts in the **Valley of the Kings**, especially in those of *Sethos I*, *Ramesses II* and *Ramesses III*. Compared to the traditional myth of **Heliopolis**, this tale gives a different version of the creation of the world. The same primeval gods appear, each one occuping the same function; but from one legend to another, the way their functions are put in place inside the universe change.

The tale starts as the gods and men live together on earth under the guardianship of the Universal Master, the god ***Re'***, and everything seems to work perfectly. However, with time, ***Re'*** is not the same man any more and his body has changed; now his bones are made of silver, his limbs of gold, and his hair of lapis-lazuli. Age is only taking its due, and that is probably the reason for which mankind decides to foment a revolt against him. Warned by his retinue of the plot against him, he summons the council of gods in the utmost secrecy. ***Shu*** and ***Tefenet***, ***Geb*** and ***Nut*** were there, and also ***Nun***, the original ocean. Of course, ***Re'*** awaits their advice: *"Here are the men born of my eye plotting against me; tell me what you would do against this"* he asks them. ***Nun*** suggests that he send his eye against the men. The other gods agree, for as they say, *"there is no eye stronger than that one"* to strike the plotters. So the decision is taken to send the eye of ***Re'*** on earth in the guise of ***Hathor***. ***Hathor*** makes herself a blood-thirsty goddess, and goes into the desert where men have found refuge, to strike terror into their hearts. But she goes even further: she exterminates a great part of the population and it ends in a blood-bath. Proud of herself, she returns to the Universal Master who praises her because, he thinks, his authority will be easier to establish now that there are fewer men.

However, ***Hathor*** seems to have enjoyed the mission a bit too much, and ***Re'*** not wanting humanity to disappear, imagines a stratagem to quench the goddess's thirst for blood. He sends messengers to **Elephantine** to bring him back *"great quantities of didi." "Didi"* is probably a kind of red ochre, or in any case, a reddening substance. In the meantime, he has his maidservants brewing a great quantity of beer. Once it is mixed with this *"didi,"* the beer looks very much like blood. Before the divine assembly, attentively looking on, this strange liquid is prepared and poured into seven thousand jars, which are to be spilled on the site of the next massacre.

Just as foreseen, the goddess ***Hathor*** arrives at dawn, well-prepared to massacre the men left on earth. What she sees surprises her: for as far as she can see, the fields are inundated with this red beer that she thinks, of course, is blood. She does not resist the desire to drink and drink more of it: and soon she is totally drunk and incapable of recognizing men, and even less of killing them. And so mankind was saved from total destruction.

But ***Re'*** is dejected. He feels old and tired. He isn't interested in living with men any more. So, for the second time, he summons the assembly of gods to tell them his spiritual plight. And then again, it is ***Nun*** who offers a solution: he asks ***Nut*** to change into a cow, and invites the solar god to sit on her back. The next morning at dawn, ***Re'*** looks down on his kingdom, and realizes that all men are armed with bows and arrows and bludgeons, ready to kill one another. Disgusted, he prays ***Nut*** to take him away from this cruel world: *"Lift me up"* he implores her. And so the cow takes the solar god towards the heavens, and she is transformed into the goddess of the sky. ***Re'*** seems happy at last; from where he is, he can see what is happening on earth. On the other hand, ***Nut*** is less satisfied: she is made dizzy by the heights. To prevent this problem, ***Re'*** creates eight spirits, who, two by two, have to hold each foot of the cow. He also asks ***Shu***, the god of space and air, to put himself under ***Nut's*** stomach, and to hold her body with his outstretched arms.

## *Satis*

Satis 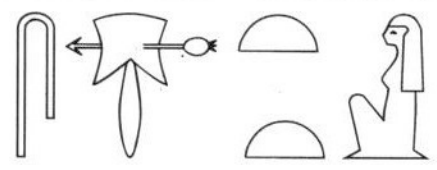

*Associated with Khnum and the infant goddess Anukis*

*Goddess guardian of the sources of the Nile and patroness of the cataract*

*Principal place of worship: Elephantine (Upper Egypt)*

*Representation: a woman wearing the crown of Upper Egypt with antelope horns on each side*

"The Lady of the island of **Sehel**", ***Satis***, is a goddess venerated in **Elephantine,** and in the surrounding islands. She is part of a triad with the potter god ***Khnum*** and the infant goddess ***Anukis.*** This association actually begins at a latter time. In the beginning, ***Satis*** is individually worshipped and, alone, she is the patroness of the cataract. During the New Kingdom very likely, she is associated with ***Khnum***; both gods, who until then have been venerated apart, are objects of a common cult in **Elephantine**. Much later, little ***Anukis*** appears and by joining the pair forms a triad. Little by little, legends include this association, which have been used since then to explain a totally incomprehensible phenomenon to the ancient Egyptians: the flood.

In an underground cave close to the first cataract, the divine family is said to reign: ***Khnum***, ***Satis*** and ***Anukis***. Every year, all three draw from the reserves and set free the proper amount of silt necessary for the fertilization of the fields and crops. It is ***Ha'py***, the spirit of the Nile, who builds up the reserves. The importance of these deities within the pantheon is due to the essential role they play in the yearly flood. So just before the flood, the farmers from all over Egypt come to **Elephantine** to ask the divine triad for an adequate flooding of the country. ***Satis*** of course becomes a deity related to fertility and abundance. Her temple is then in a strategic geographical position, directly related to her honorable function: it is exactly where the first waters of the flood appear, just before the long awaited nourishing tide becomes visible. Her iconography also recalls her essential mission. For reasons we still cannot fathom, the Egyptians seem to have always thought there is a relationship between water and antelopes. So this is why ***Satis*** was always represented as a woman wearing the white crown of Upper Egypt, with on each side, two long antelope horns.

Apart from her functions relating to the floods and the Nile, ***Satis*** also protects the region of the first cataract and defends the southern borders of Egypt. In the granite quarries of **Elephantine**, numerous inscriptions left by the workers often invoked her as goddess guardian of the place. Close to the Nubian border, she is thought to be able to push back the enemy with her arrows.

But her powers are not just reserved to the world of the living: she can also intervene in the world of the dead. In many places, the "**Pyramid Texts**" mention her name as being a deity specially devoted to the purification of the bodies of the deceased.

### Re' and the feather of Ma'at

*This small copper plate represents Re', the solar god of Heliopolis, holding in his hands the ostrich feather, which is the symbol of Ma'at. This goddess incarnates several fundamental notions: cosmic order, justice, truth and harmony created by the gods and wanted by men; in a wider sense, she represents life. Many figurines represent these two deities together, since Re' generates life, and Ma'at preserves it. Unfortunately, every day, the world faces hard trials: hostile powers, malevolent beings or cosmic enemies never cease attacking the solar god with the sole ambition of disrupting this balance. The upholding of order entails a continuous battle against the forces of chaos. This is where the uraeus comes in, proudly standing in front of Re' and Ma'at: this cobra is none other than the eye of Re', in charge of the destruction of the enemies of the sun.*

New Kingdom.

**The lioness Sakhmet**

*From the New Kingdom onwards, the goddess Sakhmet is often represented with the demiurge of Memphis, Ptah, with whom she forms a divine couple. She is depicted as a lioness wearing on her head the solar disc decorated with the cobra, since she incarnates "the Eye of Re' in fury": it is her role to get rid of the enemies of the sun, and to repel the hostile forces to the edges of the created world. In front of her sits Ptah, his body wrapped in a mummy-shaped sheath, with a false beard and wearing a tight skull cap. They both carry the ankh cross which represents the divine as its symbolizes life. The scepter of the god, and the pedestal upon which his throne is put, are decorated with the three divine emblems: the cross of life, of course, along with the scepter was which incarnates the divine and the djed pillar which represents stability and duration.*

Temple of Sethos I,
New Kingdom,
Abydos, Upper Egypt.

## *Sakhmet*

Sakhmet 

Associated with the god Ptah and the son god Nefertem

Goddess incarnating the solar eye and dangerous forces whose function is to annihilate the enemies of the sun

Principal place of worship: Memphis (Lower Egypt)

Representation: woman with a lioness head

Among the gods of the Egyptian pantheon, there are several female deities whose personalities have some of the devastating aspects of ***Sakhmet***. They are called the "dangerous goddesses" and they all symbolize a specific aspect of the solar force. Also called "the Powerful One," ***Sakhmet*** is a goddess representing the omnipotence of the sun's rays. She incarnates the flaming eye of the sun, *"the Eye of **Re'** in fury."* Her main function is to annihilate the enemies of the creator and to avoid the manifestation of the forces of chaos. In this last case, she is in charge of their destruction, so that the balance dictated by the gods and wanted by men could reign. She appears as an aggressive lioness, or simply as a lioness-headed woman, who likes wandering in the desert. But her character is very ambivalent: she incarnates the destructive force of a malevolent lioness, but once calm and quiet, she becomes a cat and adopts the appearance of the goddess ***Bastet***.

Because her fits of fury can be so tremendous, ***Sakhmet*** has to be appeased, especially during the five last days of the year, the Epagomenal Days. During these days, her wrath is let loose; and the people, afraid that the annual cycle would not come back, sing her praises and litanies and offer her presents and offerings to pacify her. In those moments, her fury is such that the creator himself cannot remain close to her without fearing for his life.

He may seem a little timorous, but it must be said that the goddess has a crew of blood-thirsty and terribly feared spirits at her disposal. These are inferior spirits, raised to blindly obey their mistress and to protect her. They are strongly bound to the vengeful aspect of the solar eye and they are supposed to be born to it. ***Sakhmet*** uses them to manifest her power and will to men and gods. They are armed with spears, arrows and knives, and they fall upon anything or anybody their mistress tells them to destroy or annihilate. When they attack, they are so quick and precise that no one can escape them. When the goddess gives the order, they scatter wars, epidemics, diseases and death. However, just as ***Sakhmet*** knows how to send catastrophes, she also has a cure for every difficulty; she then takes on the guise of one of the peaceful and healing goddesses, such as ***Mut*** for instance, and she protects the corporations of doctors and veterinary surgeons.

Her main sanctuary is in **Memphis**, where she is venerated with ***Ptah***, the creative god of the town, and ***Nefertem***, the little lotus god. This association was made later; in the beginning, each of them had his own independent cult. As years went by, they were associated in a couple and then in a triad when ***Nefertem*** became the child god of **Memphis**.

## THE DIVINE TRIADS

The triads are associations of three deities of the same town according to a traditional family scheme: god, goddess, and son god or daughter goddess. These connections probably go back to the New Kingdom; it is likely that before being associated, each one of those deities was worshipped on their own. The establishment of a triad is due to the desire of the clergy to gather together the cults of a same town. But it doesn't always happen that way. In fact, only the great religious centers used this procedure to constitute divine families that could be integrated in a mythological and cosmogonic context. The most well-known triads are those of **Memphis, Thebes**, **Elephantine, Edfu** and **Abydos.**

| | | | | | |
|---|---|---|---|---|---|
| TOWN | *MEMPHIS* | *THEBES* | *ELEPHANTINE* | *EDFU* | *ABYDOS* |
| GOD | *PTAH* | *AMUN* | *KHNUM* | *HORUS* | *OSIRIS* |
| GODDESS | *SAKHMET* | *MUT* | *SATIS* | *HATHOR* | *ISIS* |
| CHILD GOD | *NEFERTEM* | *KHONS* | *ANUKIS* | *HARSOMTUS* | *HORUS* |

## *Serket*

Serket 

*Scorpion goddess*

*Healing deity and magician protector of men against venomous bites; guardian of the dead*

*Representation: a scorpion with the head of a woman, woman with the head of a scorpion, or a scorpion*

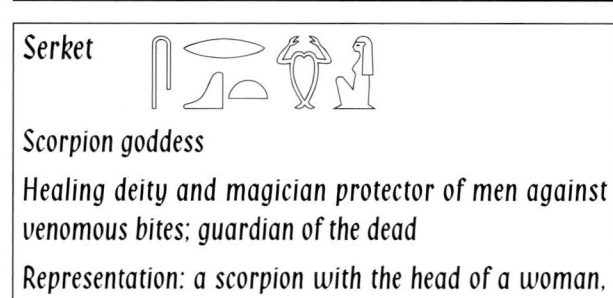

In the Egyptian religion, there are numerous fierce animals that are deified and worshipped, such as ***Taweret***, the hippopotamus goddess, or ***Sobek***, the crocodile god. This is the case with ***Serket,*** the scorpion goddess. She belongs to the group of healer or wizard deities associated with ***Isis.*** The function of ***Serket*** is double: she defends human beings on earth against all insect and snake bites, and she watches over the dead in the next world. With ***Isis, Neith*** and ***Nephthys*** she especially guards the four **canopic jars** into which the

## THE EGYPTIAN BESTIARY

| | | |
|---|---|---|
| ANTELOPE | *SATIS* | Protector of the sources of the Nile |
| BABOON | *HAPY* | Protector of the canopic jars and spirit of the North |
| | *THOTH* | God of writing, patron of scribes and divine recorder |
| BULL | *APIS* | Sacred bull of Memphis |
| CAT | *BASTET* | Daughter of Re' and peaceful goddess |
| COBRA | *WADJIT* | Tutelary goddess of Lower Egypt |
| COW | *HATHOR* | Daughter of the sun with universal capacities |
| | *NUT* | Goddess of the sky |
| CROCODILE | *SOBEK* | Lord of the waters and creative god in Crocodilopolis |
| MYTHICAL DOG | *SETH* | Ambivalent god incarnating disorder but protector of the solar boat |
| FALCON | *HAROERIS* | "Horus the Elder," defender of the solar god |
| | *HARAKHTY* | Solar god incarnating the sun at its zenith |
| | *HORUS* | Celestial god protector of the pharaonic royalty |
| | *MONTU* | Warrior god of the Theban region |
| | *QEBEHSENUF* | Protector of the canopic jars and spirit of the west |
| | *SOKAR* | Patron of craftsmen and funerary god of Memphis |
| FROG | *HEQET* | Protector of the sources of the Nile |
| GAZELLE | *ANUKIS* | Protector of homes |
| HIPPOPOTAMUS | *TAWERET* | Helper of Khnum during royal childbirths |
| IBIS | *THOTH* | God of writing, patron of scribes and divine recorder |
| JACKAL | *ANUBIS* | God of mummification |
| | *DUAMUTEF* | Protector of the Canopic jars and spirit of the east |
| LION | *SHU* | God of space, symbolizing life and vital breath |
| LIONESS | *SAKHMET* | Goddess incarnating the solar eye and dangerous powers |
| | *TEFENET* | Daughter of Re' representing cosmic order and heat |
| RAM | *AMUN* | State god from the Middle Kingdom |
| | *KHNUM* | Guardian of the sources of the Nile and creative god in Esna |
| | *RE'* | Solar god and creative god in Heliopolis |
| SCARAB | *KHEPRI* | Solar creative god in Heliopolis representing the rising sun |
| SCORPION | *SERKET* | Healing goddess and magician |
| SNAKE | *APOPHIS* | Cosmic enemy symbolizing the forces of destruction |
| SPHINX | *HARMAKHIS* | "Horus on the Horizon," one of the forms of the solar god |
| | *HURUN* | Canaanite god, assimilated into Harmakhis |
| VULTURE | *MUT* | Wife of Amun, sometimes assimilated into Sakhmet |
| | *NEKHBET* | Tutelary goddess of Upper Egypt |

viscera of the deceased are placed: she watches over the intestines with ***Qebehsenuf,*** the spirit of the West. In the "**Legend of Osiris**," she is the one who takes charge of little ***Horus***, who is hidden by his mother in the Delta marshes to escape from ***Seth.*** However, she cannot prevent ***Horus*** from being bitten by one of her fellow scorpions; fortunately the united magic powers of ***Isis*** and ***Thoth***, the god of sciences, will be able to rid the body of the little god of the venom.

Actually, in spite of her terrifying appearance, ***Serket*** is a kindly goddess. The priests attached to her cult are supposed to be wonderful magicians and excellent doctors, the practice of both activities being quite compatible. It is told that they are very good at curing insect attacks, any kinds of bites and scorpion stings; they know which medication has to be prescribed, whether for immediate relief or against eventual secondary effects. In most cases, ***Serket*** is represented as a scorpion with the head of a woman, as a woman wearing a scorpion on her head, or simply just as a scorpion. The hieroglyphic sign, likewise, that designates her is simply a scorpion. In certain drawings, the animal is presented without its poisonous tail and its head, probably with the intention of magically making it powerless.

It must be said that in the tombs, the signs and objects represented on the walls are supposed to come to life if the right magic words are spoken. Thus, by amputating the scorpion of its head and tail, it is made harmless forever.

**Serket the scorpion**

*At first sight, Serket may seem to be unsympathetic because of her repellent appearance. But, in fact, there is nothing of that: she is a beneficient goddess as she intervenes as a protector against bites and stings of all kind. Serket is often represented as a woman with a scorpion on her head. When the artist wants to insist on her healing qualities, he will probalby use the iconography of this statuette, in which the scorpion is more obvious. Serket here is wearing Hathor's crown with two cow horns and the solar disc.*

Late Period.

**Sarapis**

*The iconography of Sarapis is much more Greek than Egyptian. This is due to the fact that he appears only in the later days in Egypt. It was the pharaohs of Greek descent, the Ptolemies, who create Sarapis, and who give him many qualities borrowed from Egyptian and Greek deities: Osiris, Apis, Pluto, Asklepios... He has long hair and a beard, he wears a tunic and sandals. In some representations, he carries objects that identify him immediately, such as the calathos or the horn of plenty. This statue has no particular detail, so it is difficult to be sure of his identity. However, everything seems to show that it is really Sarapis.*

Ptolemaic Period.

# *Sarapis*

Sarapis

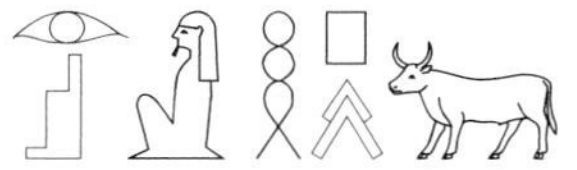

Associated with Isis and the son god Harpokrates

Funerary and agrarian god; healing god; protector of the Ptolemies and of the town of Alexandria

Principal place of worship: Alexandria (Lower Egypt)

Representation: a bearded with long hair; man clothed as a Greek and wearing a crown named the calathos (a measure of seeds)

**Plutarch** tells us of a legend about the apparition of ***Sarapis*** in Egypt. *Ptolemy I* would have seen in a dream a colossal statue of a god who lived in **Sinope**, a town on the Black Sea. This strange deity would have asked him to transfer her image to **Alexandria,** that is what he did. When it got there, the priests and wise men identified the statue as the representation of ***Pluto***. It was given the name of **Sarapis,** which *"for the Egyptian corresponds to Pluto, the god of Hades or hell."* It is clear that it was a way of introducing a fully Greek god into the Egyptian pantheon.

But in fact ***Sarapis*** is not an importation, but a mere creation. He didn't exist before, and was created by the *Ptolemies* to help the interests of the new political regime. The iconography of ***Sarapis*** recalls his fathers origin: it is inspired by ***Zeus*** and only a few details show any Egyptian tradition. ***Sarapis*** sits majestically, draped in a long tunic and his feet in sandals. He has long hair and a beard and he wears on his head either the **calathos**, which is a Greek name that designates a measure of seeds, or the atef crown of ***Osiris***. Sometimes he holds a scepter or a horn of plenty, and sometimes little ***Harpokrates*** or the dog **Cerberus** are next to him. However, whatever variations are brought to his representations, he is essentially depicted as a Greek god.

Many specialists have pondered over one of the main questions concerning ***Sarapis***: who is he actually? To begin with, the context in which he appears is very particular, since the country already has many gods of all kinds. In order to rally Egyptian people to his cult, he needs to have an original personality able to avoid any competition with the local deities. **Plutarch** once more enlightens us on his real nature: *"the priests say that **Osiris** and **Apis** were united in one entity."* The real name of ***Sarapis*** is ***"Osor-Hapi"***, a combination of the names of ***Osiris*** and ***Apis***.

***Sarapis*** has several functions. He is first of all a funerary god; but as ***Osiris*** has been the god of the deceased for all Egyptians for a very long time, ***Sarapis*** appears in this role to be just a Greek version of the great funerary god. His **calathos** and horn of plenty show that he is a god related to agrarian fertility, a very common theme in the Egyptian pantheon. But ***Sarapis*** gives very popular oracles: he predicts the amount of crops the farmers will have, and gives them advice for their work. But above all, and there he is excellent, ***Sarapis*** is a healing god; this talent is not attributed to any particular deity in ancient Egypt, but many different deities possess it. So ***Sarapis*** eventually becomes the master of this specialty, and it is said that in his sanctuary of **Canope**, a small town close to **Alexandria**, there are many miraculous healings. And last but not least, ***Sarapis*** appears as the protector of the *Ptolemaic* dynasty and of the city of **Alexandria**. He is then associated with ***Isis,*** who is tremendously popular, and then with the child ***Harpokrates***; the three of them become a divine triad that guarantees royal balance.

## Correlation between Egyptian and Greek Mythology
### (according to Plutarch and Herodotus)

| | | | | | |
|---|---|---|---|---|---|
| ***Amun*** | Zeus | ***Isis*** | Demeter | ***Wadjit*** | Laertes |
| ***Bastet*** | Artemis | ***Khons*** | Hercules | ***Ptah*** | Hephaestus |
| ***Goat of Mendès*** | Pan | ***Min*** | Perseus | ***Sarapis*** | Pluto |
| ***Hathor*** | Aphrodite | ***Neith*** | Athena | ***Seth*** | Typhon |
| ***Horus*** | Apollo | ***Osiris*** | Dionysos | ***Thoth*** | Hermes |

# Seshat

> Seshat
>
> 
>
> *First assistant and sometimes the companion of Thoth, the god of writing.*
>
> *Patroness of scribes and schoolchildren; goddess of science and mathematics; mistress of the royal records; trustee of the architectural drawings*
>
> *Representation: a woman wearing a rosette with seven branches crowned with two overturned horns*

The different functions that are held by ***Seshat*** are all connected to her role as archivist, scientist and mathematician. Her names mean "the lady scribe," and she is so precise and skillful with her paintbrush and her reed that she soon becomes the preferred assistant of the god of writing, ***Thoth***. Some traditions even present her as ***Thoth***'s wife. At his side, she is the patroness of scribes and schoolchildren, and she particularly watches over the royal institutions which train the children who will be the future scribes.

She is depicted as a young woman, sometimes wearing a leopard's skin, and always having on her head a symbol for which we still don't have a any satisfactory explanation. It is a rosette with seven branches, above which are two overturned horns. In some texts, this symbol on its own is enough to identify her. An enigmatic man from the late Roman period called **Horapollo**, who wrote a study on hieroglyphs, and relates this symbol to destiny, because it is ***Seshat*** who predicts a long reign with many jubilees for the Pharaoh. This ritual, called the **Heb-Sed** or the **Sed-Feast**, is aimed at regenerating by magic the physical strength and the abilities of the king. On this occasion, the Pharaoh visits the main shrines of Upper and Lower Egypt, where he practises certain rites aimed at renewing power, might and strength: archery, running, hunting and all kinds of trials which are there to show that he has lost none of his former strength. This festival is usually celebrated in the 30th year of a king's effective reign. However, calculations tend to prove that it is celebrated at shorter intervals, since some pharaohs instigate several jubilees during their reign: as did *Amenhotep III* or *Ramesses II* for instance. So if the goddess ***Seshat*** predicts many jubilees for a king, it is interpreted as a good omen. She is also the one who is in charge of the royal records methodically registering all the important royal deeds and essential features of each reign. During the coronation festivities, she registers with ***Thoth*** the five names chosen by Pharaoh. Punctually, she counts the years of life and of reign of the pharaohs, so that the "**royal lists**" could be written. These documents, unfortunately too rare, are a very important source of documentation for the reconstitution of a coherent Egyptian chronology. Most of these lists go back to the Ramessid Period, particularly to the reigns of *Sethos I* and *Ramesses II*: for instance, there are the "**King List of Abydos**," the "**Turin Royal Canon**" or the "**Table of Saqqara**." They list the names of all the pharaohs acknowledged as their legitimate predecessors since the foundation of the kingdom of Egypt. In short, ***Seshat*** registers all the deeds and important facts of the pharaonic royalty. She is the goddess of writing and mathematics, the mistress of libraries and archives.

She also plays an essential part in the foundation ceremonies of religious buildings. In the Egyptian tradition, the construction of a temple requires the assistance of many different people, without whom absolutely nothing could be done.

The ritual is very complex, and needs the participation of the king as well as a few very specific deities. As she is patroness of the building plans and trustee of architectural drawings, ***Seshat*** assists and advises the king during the conception and the construction of the sanctuary. She controls the marking on the ground and makes sure that the laying out of the construction is properly made. This job is made by the pharaoh at night, as the angles of the building have to be properly oriented. To do this, the king uses a device that allows him to fix the exact location of the future building, depending on the position of the stars. ***Seshat***, who is eminent in the science of astronomy, checks the right orientation and, once all this has been done, conjectures on the stability of the building: *"As true as your building is as solid on its foundations as the sky on its props, your work shall last with its master as the earth lasts with the divine ennead... It will not know destruction on earth forever..."* Then the excavation for the foundation can be started and walls constructed all being placed under the protection of other deities.

**Seshat, the Mistress of Books**

*The goddess Seshat can be identified by the insignia she wears on her head, a rosette with seven equal branches crowned with two overturned horns. The real signification of this emblem is still unexplained; according to some sources, it has a direct relationship with destiny. Whatever it is, it is a characteristic symbol of Seshat: it appears in the hieroglyphs of her name, as on all her representations. The only translation of her name meaning "the lady scribe," corroborates her functions: actually, her role is to write, calculate, record, look after the schoolchildren, draw plans, protect the scribes... She likes to be represented on the wall of the temples performing these official functions. On this relief of the great temple of Abu Simbel, Seshat is completing the royal archives, with her writing reed in one hand and an inkwell in the other.*

Temple of Ramesses II,
New Kingdom,
Abu Simbel, Upper Egypt.

# Seth

Seth 

*Son of Geb, the earth, and Nut, the sky*

*Brother of Osiris, Isis, Horus the Elder, and Nephthys*

*Uncle of Horus*

*Double-faced deity: god of evil and thunder, responsible for trouble and disorder, but also protector of the solar boat*

*Representation: mythical animal or a man with the head of this animal*

***Seth*** incarnates on his own the whole ambiguity of divinity. Due to his double personality, his destiny changes through history, according to the reigning dynasty. His iconography recalls his ambiguous character: he is represented as a mythical animal (the Sethian animal) of mixed breed, or as a man with the head of that animal. We can observe a greyhound-like body, with a long forked tail, a slender and aquiline muzzle, and straight long beveled ears. His part in the "**Legend of Osiris**" makes him a god of evil: not only does he kill his brother, but he has no scruples about fighting ***Horus*** to usurp his title of king. He is then associated with images of storm, violence and tempest. He is also, in a more general fashion, an instigator of trouble and confusion. His domain is the desert, because it symbolizes the foreigner, the invader, and generally what everyone considers as hostile. But, at the same time, he is the protector of the boat of ***Re'***, the solar god; he is in charge of repelling the incessant attacks of the snake ***Apophis***, in order to maintain universal balance. Armed with his spear or his knife, he throws himself against the monster of darkness to save cosmic harmony. Some sovereigns elevate him to the highest grade in the Egyptian pantheon. The Ramessid dynasty, that originally comes from **Avaris**, the town of ***Seth***, gives him such importance, that some of the kings, the *Sethos* in particular, don't hesitate adding his name to their own. However, this triumph does not last long; from the Late Period on, he is abhorred and hated. Hymns chant his defeat against ***Horus***, and his name is systematically chiseled out, because he acquires devilish connotations.

In the ancient theology of **Memphis**, which is the capital of the country under the Old Kingdom, it is said that the king inherits Lower Egypt through ***Horus***, and Upper Egypt through ***Seth***: in equal parts, the "Two Lords" transmit to him their respective force and throne. With the introduction of the Osirian myth, ***Horus*** becomes the universal master of earth, and relegates ***Seth*** back to lesser functions. This victory is the issue of a long struggle between ***Horus***, who inherits the earthly kingdom through his father, and ***Seth***, the murderer of ***Osiris***.

Indeed, the difficult problem about the murder of ***Osiris*** is his succession to the throne of Egypt. ***Seth*** ascends to the throne by force, but ***Horus***, with the help of his mother ***Isis***, claimed royalty as his, because he is the son of ***Osiris***. So it is up to the court of gods to settle the dispute. The sessions are presided by the creative god, called the "Universal Master," and conducted by the secretary of the gods, Thoth, who introduces the debate by giving the grievances held against ***Seth***. It is interesting to note that when the tale starts, the trial has already lasted eighty years. Some of the members of the tribunal mark their preference for ***Horus*** who is, according to royalty, the sole legitimate heir to the crown. The assembly of gods approves, but the Universal Master, who prefers not to antagonize ***Seth*** whose strength he values, takes offense: *"How is it that you decide on your own?"* To pacify him, a member of the divine jury offers to ask an outsider for advice; and it is decided to consult ***Neith***, the goddess of **Sais**, well-known for her profound wisdom. In her answer to ***Thoth***'s letter, she sides with ***Horus***, but proposes to offer ***Seth*** as a compensation the goddesses ***Anta*** and ***Astarte*** as wives. Satisfied with this proposal, the divine court rejoices, but the Universal Master, who would like to see ***Seth*** win, underlines that ***Horus*** is too young and has too little experience to assume the heavy responsibility of the kingdom.

Then ***Baba***, an obscure god belonging to the entourage of ***Osiris***, steps in, and furiously dares to insult the Universal Master, by telling him he has no authority and that he does not know how to be respected. Terribly wounded, the creative god leaves the audience and retires into his palace in great dignity. As the sessions cannot go on without him, ***Hathor*** decides to react. She knows of the roguish inclinations of her father, and to make him smile, she presents herself in front of him; she lifts her skirts and shows him what is underneath. The expected

**Seth against Apophis**

*Most of the funerary books refer to the trips of the sun, Re', through the sky. These daily travels from west to east, and from east to west, are made aboard a boat upon which the sun and the crew embark. But regularly, a monster appears from the depths of the darkness, and attacks the solar boat, trying to sink it: it is Apophis, a giant and terrifying snake who incarnates the malevolent powers. At the bow of the ship stands Seth, ready to intervene at each new attack. As soon as the monster of destruction appears, Seth throws himself upon it, and cuts it with his spear or his knife and sends it back to the ends of the world. This perpetual struggle symbolizes the triumph of an organized world upon chaos, of order upon disorder. The fight against Apophis becomes a recurrent theme in Egyptian iconography. Sometimes as here, the scene of the fight has been taken out of its context to appear alone: the solar boat and its crew have disappeared; there is only Seth left, or a fabulous animal that represents him, locked in struggle wth the snake.*

Tomb 359 of Inerkhaû, Deir el-Medina, New Kingdom, West Thebes, Upper Egypt.

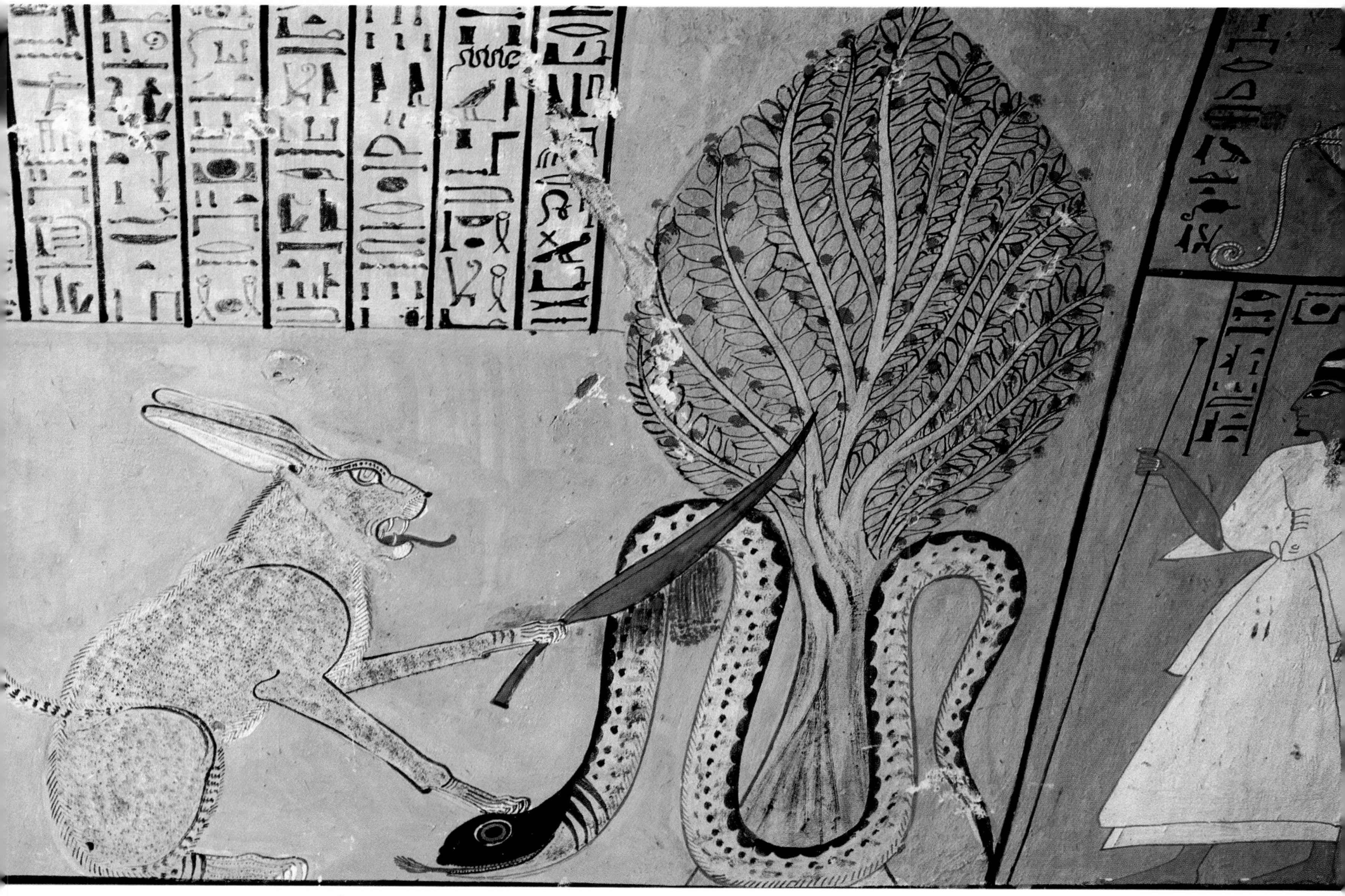


reaction is immediate: the Universal Master comes back and the trial goes on with ***Seth*** and ***Horus*** tirelessly defending there own case.

Exasperated by all this shuffling, ***Isis*** proposes to *"put these words in front of* ***Atum****, the powerful prince who stays in* ***Heliopolis****, and in front of* ***Khepri****, who resides in his boat."* This interference infuriates ***Seth***, who refuses to continue the contest in the presence of ***Isis***. Surrendering to ***Seth***'s whim, the Universal Master invites the court to carry on the session in a more protected place, where the goddess would not be let in, called "the Island of the Middle." To do this, he asks the ferryman **Anti** to refuse to take any woman who looks like ***Isis*** to the island. But ***Isis*** refuses to abandon her son, and decides to disobey the Universal Master. She disguises herself as an old woman, and gets the ferry man to take her to the island in return for a gold ring. Once over on the island, she turns into a beautiful young girl, aiming to catch ***Seth***'s attention to set a trap for him... And indeed, attracted by her charms, the unfortunate fellow lets himself be maneuvered by the goddess. During the conversation, he even finally admits that the rights of succession should go to a direct descendant rather than any other person. Then ***Isis*** triumphantly changes herself into a hawk and thus reveals her true identity to him. ***Seth***, realizing how naïve he has been, goes to see the Universal Master who cannot give him satisfaction, and because of the rash declarations ***Seth*** has made, gives the crown of Egypt to ***Horus***. But the story does not end there, as ***Seth*** seems to be quite intent on getting his revenge. He then invites ***Horus*** to join in a competition, during which they would transform themselves into hippopotami and dive into the water; of course the one who would stay the longest under water would be the winner. ***Isis***, present at the contest, is unable to prevent herself from helping her son by handicapping his competitor. She throws a first harpoon that hits ***Horus***. She takes the spear out and starts the maneuver all over again; then, she hits ***Seth*** with all her strenght. However, feeling remorse, she pities the wounded and she takes the spear out. Infuriated by this gesture of pity, ***Horus*** cuts his mother's head off, carries her body into the mountains, and turns her into a statue of silex. This event rouses the Universal Master's wrath; he tells the deities of the Ennead to bring ***Horus*** back to **Heliopolis** to punish him. Of course, it is ***Seth*** who finds ***Horus*** first. He throws himself upon him, tears his eyes out, and buries them in the hill. They instantly turn into bright stars. As ***Hathor*** has no news from ***Horus***, she sets off to look for him. She finds him abandoned and crying. To give him his sight back, she pours milk from a gazelle into his eye sockets and takes him to the Universal Master. Tired of all these quarrels, the creative god asks the two enemies to make peace around a banquet.

So ***Seth*** invites ***Horus*** to diner. After the meal, ***Seth*** tries to rape him, and ***Horus*** manages to collect a little of ***Seth***'s semen in his hands. He comes back to his mother to tell her about the doings of ***Seth***. ***Isis***, horrified, cuts his hands off, throws them in the water, and gives him new hands. She then asks ***Horus*** to give her a little of his own semen, which she sprinkles over the salads of ***Seth***'s vegetable garden. As he does every evening, ***Seth*** eats some salad and thus is fecundated by ***Horus***'s semen. He has of course no idea of this trap. He asks for a gathering of the council of gods, with the intention of making fun of ***Horus***: *"Give me the title of king... Because, concerning **Horus** right here, I acted as a male with him."* At this revelation, the gods make fun of ***Horus***, who calmly asks ***Thoth*** to examine the two seminal liquids to check where they come from. To the astonishment of the divine assembly, ***Seth***'s semen comes from water, whereas ***Horus***'s comes from ***Seth***.

Despite all these episodes, ***Seth,*** more decided than ever, hopes to take the title away from ***Horus*** by giving him a last challenge; both should get into stone boats for a race, and the prize for the winner would be the throne of Egypt. But ***Horus*** secretly makes a wooden boat, which he covers with plaster to camouflage it. Of course, during the race, only ***Horus***'s boat does not sink. Furious, ***Seth*** changes into a hippopotamus and overturns his challenger's boat. ***Horus*** manages to swim to the riverbank, and he goes to **Sais** to talk to the goddess ***Neith*** asking her to interfere to put an end to this neverending quarrel. In **Heliopolis**, each one agrees that ***Horus***'s grievances are justified. But as if even more arguments were needed, ***Thoth*** offers to consult ***Osiris***, the father of ***Horus***. In his answer, ***Osiris*** declares that he cannot understand this animosity against his son. He explains that his rights are indisputable. He even threatens the supreme court. As god of vegetation, he says, he can deprive Egypt of all its resources; and as god of the Underworld, he can send on earth emissaries of death to punish injustice and lies. The gods feel directly concerned by the words of ***Osiris***, and quickly decide to give a favorable verdict to ***Horus***. The Universal Master summons ***Seth*** and makes him acknowledge the exclusive rights of ***Horus*** on the Egyptian kingdom. Therefore, ***Horus*** solemnly inherits his father's throne. As for ***Seth***, he is given to the Universal Master to sit by him in his company: *"He shall howl in the sky and will be feared."*

## *Shu*

Shu 

Son of Re'-Atum-Khepri, the sun

Brother and husband of Tefenet, the heat

Father of Geb, the earth, and Nut, the sky

God of air symbolizing the vital breath

Representation: man sometimes wearing a feather on his head

***Shu*** belongs, with his sister ***Tefenet***, to the first generation of gods of the great Ennead of **Heliopolis**. It is told that they are both born from the spittle of the demiurge, the god ***Atum***. This explanation probably comes from a simple play on words between the names of the two deities, ***Shu*** and ***Tefenet***, and the roots of two Egyptian terms that mean to "spit," *ishesh* and *tef*. ***Shu*** is a god of air, born to allow ***Atum*** to *"see what he had created."* This space of air, very badly defined, represents the vital breath and the space allowing the sun's light to diffuse. As for ***Tefenet***, she completes her brother's functions by bringing heat and cosmic order. At this stage, creation is at its very beginning, since ***Geb*** and ***Nut***, the sky and earth, have not yet been begotten.

**The "Lions of the horizon"**

*This iconography of Shu and Tefenet is a reference to a very particular aspect of their personality. They are depicted as two lions with their backs to each other, carrying Re', the sun, on their shoulders. Everyday, it is their duty to beget the sun, which itself has begotten them. This apparent contradiction is explained by the fact that the sun is only revealed through his children: it is up to Shu and Tefenet to distribute the rays of the sun. From this point of view, the three of them are inseparable. Shu and Tefenet only exist because Re' brought them to life; and Re' only exists because Shu and Tefenet are the mediums for his energy and thus allow him to manifest himself.*

Tomb 5 of Nefer-Abu, Deir el-Medina, New Kingdom, West Thebes Upper Egypt

These two divine principles have to be interpreted as emanations of the sun that transmit its radiation, according to their different functions. A detailed analysis of the cosmogonic tales actually shows that it is their presence that gives the sun its complete measure. It is ***Shu*** and ***Tefenet*** who give reality to the demiurge, and give him the opportunity to reveal himself: *"The one who lives, **Tefenet**, is my daughter who shall exist with her brother **Shu**... I live with my two children. I live with my two fledgelings, while I am with them in their heart, one before me and one behind me."* ***Shu*** and ***Tefenet*** are therefore totally inseparable. Every morning, their role is to give birth to the sun, of which they are supposed to be the children. In the religious iconography, this particular aspect of their personality is represented by two lions back to back, the "lions of the horizon," carrying the sun on their shoulders.

The sequel of the tale of the Heliopolitan cosmogony throws light on one of the main roles of the god ***Shu***. We have seen how the sun emerged from ***Nun***, and how it gave birth to ***Shu*** and ***Tefenet***. Afterwards, to make the creation perfect, these two deities mate to give birth to ***Geb*** and ***Nut***, the sky and earth, who themselves can only mate secretly. Displeased about this relationship, the demiurge orders ***Shu*** to interfere. He decides to separate them, leaving ***Geb*** on earth, and sending ***Nut*** into the celestial heights. He then becomes the space separating these two elements: a space that allows the full diffusion of light, the total expression of his father, the universal god. Many documents illustrate this stage of the creation and depict ***Shu***, with his arms lifted, maintaining the slim body of ***Nut*** high above ***Geb***, languidly lying on the earth. Very often, the god ***Shu***, true symbol of life, carries in his hands and over his arms the **ankh cross**, which in hieroglyphic writing simply means: "Life".

A short excerpt of the legend of ***Re'*** explains how the division of time was organized afterwards. The story tells how men fomented a revolt against the tired and aging god, who decided to leave earth without, however, depriving it of his light. Only as he wasn't as strong as he used to be in his youth, he established a cycle that would allow him to rejuvenate regularly; he would light the world during the day, would disappear in the evening to search for his own resources, and once rested, he would reappear at dawn as powerful as the day before. This organization settles for ever the cycles of days and nights of the sun, and by extension, the calendar and the cyclical movements of time.

*Following pages*

**The Ani Papyrus**

*Measuring about 78 feet, the Ani's Papyrus is one of the longest works of this kind that we know about. Along the columns of writing and drawings, appear the numerous chapters of the "Book of the Dead." This funerary book gives the deceased a series of formulas that are supposed to ensure his resurrection. During his journey, the deceased meets the funerary divinities and spirit he must recognize, so that they let him pass allowing him to continue his journey in the winding paths of the Underworld. Here, Ani and his wife are playing Senet, a game similar to chess, while in front of them, their souls, depicted as birds, contemplate a cosmic scene: the "lions of the horizon," Shu and Tefenet, carrying their father, the sun, on their shoulders. Above their heads is the celestial vault, symbolized by a long black line curved at each end.*

New Kingdom

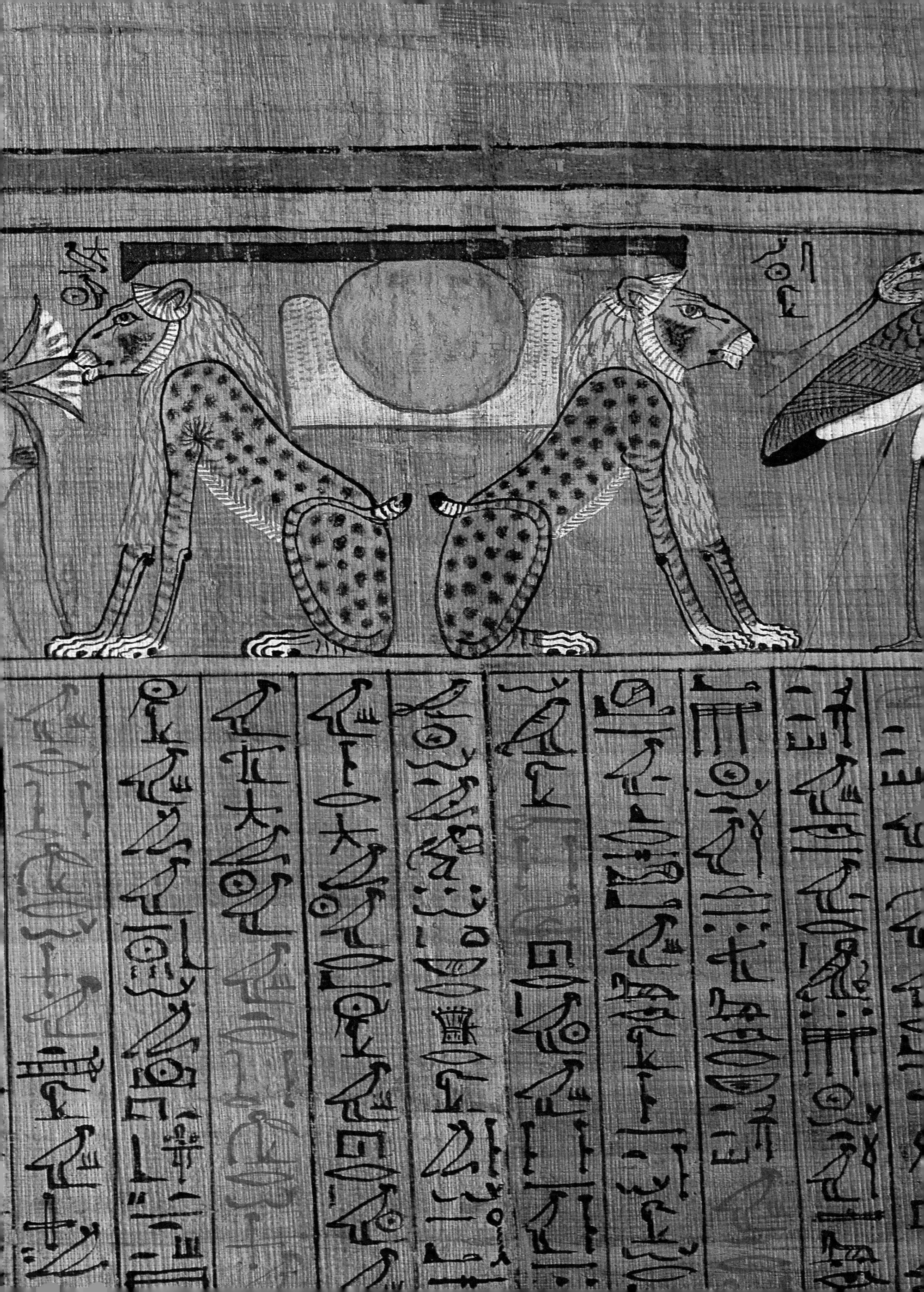

## Sobek

Sobek 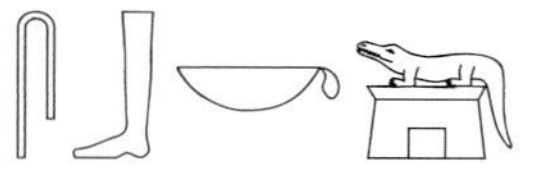

Son of the goddess Neith (Sais); associated in triad with the goddess Hathor and the god son Khons (Kom-Ombo)

Lord of the Waters; creative god as Sobek-Re'

Principal places of worship: Kom-Ombo (Upper Egypt) and Crocodilopolis (el-Faiyum oasis)

Representation: crocodile or man with the head of a crocodile

In the beginning, ***Sobek***, the crocodile god, is the Lord of the Waters. All the marshes, lakes, rivers and canals are under his guardianship. This is why his main places of worship are directly on the Nile or in spots with plenty of water, such as the Delta of the Nile or in the oasis of **el-Faiyum**. A popular belief credits him with the qualities of a god of fertility; it was told that the more crocodiles in the river, the bigger the flood would be, and thus the more plentiful the crops. Later, his personality acquires solar characteristics: he becomes ***Sobek-Re'***, a universal creative god. Every morning, he is greeted with these words: *"Greetings to you, Sobekfrom Crocodilopolis, Re', Horus, powerful god. Greetings to you, Sobek from Crocodilopolis. Greetings to you who comes from the original waters, Horus master of Egypt. Bull of the bulls, great male being, Master of the floating islands."*

In **Sais**, where he is considered to be the son of ***Neith***, he is the one who *"makes the vegetation grow on the river banks."* In the southern part of the country, he is in possession of a very popular cult at **Ombos**, the actual site of **Kom-Ombo**, where he shares his temple with ***Haroeris*** "***Horus the Great***." It is here that every year the flood is celebrated. The conception of this temple, dictated by the need to honor two deities in the same place, is unusual and unique in Egypt. The architects chose to preserve the usual plan of a religious building, but doubling all the spaces: two main axes lead to two sanctuaries, the whole temple being surrounded by only one wall. Here ***Sobek*** is associated in triad with ***Hathor*** and ***Khons***, and the texts explain the integration of the gods of **Ombos** in the cosmogonic system of **Heliopolis**: in **Kom-Ombo**, ***Re'*** appears as ***Sobek*** and ***Shu*** as ***Haroeris.***

In the oasis of **el-Faiyum,** many sanctuaries are dedicated to ***Sobek*** in **Crocodilopolis** and close to the lake **Moeris**. He very often has other names: he is ***Pneferos*** "the one with the beautiful face," ***Soknopaios*** "***Sobek*** master of the island"... But all these names evoke just one god, the crocodile ***Sobek***, and testify the great love of the inhabitants of a village for their own form of god. Just as in other sanctuaries in Egypt consecrated to ***Sobek***, the god here can appear to his worshippers in the guise of an animal. **Herodotus** writes about these customs: *"Close to Thebes and the lake Moeris, the sacred character of the crocodile is particularly recognized: each region chooses a crocodile and feeds it. The animal is tamed: earrings made out of gold and glass are put into its ears and bracelets on its forefeet. While it lives, it is given special food and is cared for; once it dies, it is embalmed and laid into a sacred tomb."*

## Sokar

Sokar 

Patron of the blacksmiths and funerary deity

Principal place of worship: Memphis (Lower Egypt)

Representation: a mummy with the head of a hawk

***Sokar*** is a god worshipped in the town of **Memphite** necropolis from the oldest times. In the beginning, he shares with ***Ptah*** the protection of the craftsmen: ***Ptah*** is patron of the work of stone and wood, whereas ***Sokar*** is related to metal. He thus becomes the protector of the blacksmiths and the creator of metallurgy. ***Sokar*** is also a funerary god as he is the god of the Memphite necropolis. He reigns as master of the kingdom of **Rosetau**, *"the door of the galleries,"* which certainly means the entrance to the underground world. However, towards the end of the Old Kingdom, ***Sokar*** loses part of his importance, outdistanced by ***Ptah*** and ***Osiris*** who have stronger personalities. ***Ptah*** assumes ***Sokar***'s funerary qualities under the name of ***Ptah-Sokar***. Later, when ***Osiris*** becomes the only god of the dead in the whole Egyptian pantheon, ***Sokar*** becomes ***Ptah-Sokar-Osiris***, and definitely loses his original qualities. ***Sokar*** is generally depicted as a mummy with the head of a hawk. Sometimes, he appears as a hawk sitting in a boat decorated at the front with the head of an antelope. This iconography recalls an ancient ceremony during which ***Sokar***, standing on his boat, played an important part. The exact development of the festival is unknown, but it probably happened outside the walls of **Memphis** and had to be related to the royal office.

**The crocodile Sobek**

*The sanctuary in Kom-Ombo is divided in two very distinct parts separated by an east-west axis: the southern part is reserved to the cult of the crocodile god, Sobek, the northern part to the hawk god, Haroeris. In this sanctuary, Sobek is associated in triad with the goddess Hathor and the son god Khons. Here on this picture, he appears with his wife. It would be very difficult to recognize Hathor if her name hadn't been engraved above her head. She wears a crown that is a mixture of several divine headdresses, but that doesn't specifically identify her: the goddess here could easily be mistaken for Isis or Mut. As for Sobek, he is depicted here in a very traditional fashion; he is a man with the head of a crocodile, carrying in his left hand the was scepter of the male divinities and in his right hand the ankh cross.*

Temple of Sobek and Haroeris, Ptolemaic Period, Kom-Ombo, Upper Egypt.

# Sopdet

Sopdet 

*Incarnation of the star Sirius*

*Goddess associated with Isis*

*Deity linked to the flood, fertility and the beginning of the world*

*Representation: a bright star, a cow or a woman with the features of Isis*

Amongst all the stars and constellations registered in the sky by the Egyptians, only a few of them were deified. ***Re'*** and ***Thoth*** incarnate the sun and the moon. ***Osiris*** symbolizes the constellation of **Orion**, and ***Horus*** appears as a manifestation of the five known planets; **Mars** is called "**the Red Horus**." But in certain astronomical scenes painted on the ceilings of the royal tombs, the constellations and planets can in fact be considered as deities. The most beautiful example can be found in the tomb of *Sethos I*, in the **Valley of the Kings**. On a dark blue background symbolizing the sky, hundreds of animals are entangled, with celestial gods and goddesses wearing little solar discs or colored stars on their heads, sometimes with a small legend giving their names and qualities. Unfortunately these maps of the sky, most of them too adorned, are not always very easy to interpret. The stars are thought to be the incarnations of the souls of the deceased, and only ***Sopdet*** has the benefit of a personal cult, because she heralds the beginning of the flood. ***Sopdet*** is the name given by the Egyptians to **Sirius**, which belongs to the constellation of **Canis Major**. It is the brightest star in the sky but, more than that, it has a very particular characteristic, linked to the calendar and the flood.

The Ancient Egyptians use two calendars: the lunar calendar, reserved for religious festivities and the civil solar calendar. The civil calendar includes twelve months of thirty days, to which are added five days, the Epagomenal Days, dedicated to ***Osiris***, ***Isis***, ***Horus the Elder***, ***Seth*** and ***Nephthys***, which gives a total of three hundred and sixty five days. Three seasons of four months punctuate the year: **Akhet** (flood from June to October), **Peret** (sowing time, from November to February) and **Chemu** (harvests, from March to June).

Each month of thirty days is divided into three periods of ten days, each one of twenty four hours. The Egyptians made the year start with the first day of the flood, and they soon realized that this day was marked by an astronomical phenomenon: on that date, ***Sopdet*** appeared in the sky at the same time as the sun. This phenomenon is called the heliacal rising of **Sirius,** and was used as the beginning of the Egyptian year. So the year started with a natural phenomenon, which was the flood, and an astronomical phenomenon, which was the rise of **Sirius,** on July 19th.

However the solar year actually has three hundred and sixty five days and one fourth. In our calendars, this quarter of a day is caught up every four years with the leap-year, a trick the Egyptians didn't know about. So every four years, the Egyptian year was twenty four hours late, and it was only after one thousand four hundred and sixty years, which is a period named sothiac, that the three phenomena (the sun rise, the rise of **Sirius** and the beginning of the flood) happened all at the same time, on the first day of the year. So the error grew bigger and bigger, until the summer festivals were celebrated in winter, or the other way around. Luckily, some cautious scribes recorded in several instances the difference between the rise of **Sirius** and the beginning of the legal year. Thanks to all these notes, historians have been able to establish fixed dates that enable them to define with great accuracy the chronological foundations of Egyptian history.

From this point of view, the importance of ***Sopdet*** is easier to understand. She is closely connected with the rising of the Nile, flood and fertility. It is said she presides over the beginning of the world, since the sky, at the moment of the heliacal rising of **Sirius,** is considered to be as it was when the world was created. So, for her features, she is associated with ***Isis*** and depicted as one of the manifestations of the universal goddess. She has several iconographies: she sometimes appears as a cow, sometimes she is depicted as ***Isis,*** and sometimes she is represented as a bright yellow star. The importance of ***Sopdet*** is so great that her cult is carried on in the Nile Valley, even after the introduction of the Roman calendar taking into account the quarter of a day of the real solar year. According to ancient historians, her rise still marks *"the beginning or main part of the year."*

**The sky and the stars**

*The astronomical scenes represented in the tombs show the importance of the cosmos in Egyptian religion. This is due to the fact that Re', the solar creative god, travels through the sky. Everything is organized around him, and most funerary and sacred compositions describe his qualities, his transformations, his attributes, his journey and his nature. So the observation of the solar cycle leads to an interest in the other stars in the sky, and particularly in the constellations. The extent of Egyptian knowledge in astronomy is hard to determine, because the representations are not always very clear. However, we know that they located and deified a number of stars, especially Sopdet. According to the importance of the tombs and of their occupant, the representations are more or less complex and detailed. Sometimes, as in this representation from the tomb of Nebenma'at, they are summarized in a small vignette showing the deceased in adoration of the sun, the stars and the sky. Sometimes they completely cover the ceilings of the tombs, as in the vault of Sethos I or Ramesses VI.*

Tombe 219 de Nebenmaât, Deir el-Medina, New Kingdom, West Thebes, Upper Egypt.

# *Tanen*

*Tanen* 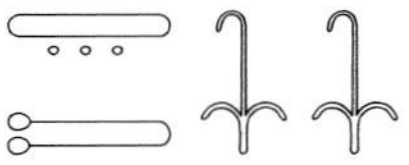

*Associated with Ptah under the name of Ptah-Tanen*

*According to the Memphite tradition, he incarnates the Primeval Mound emerging from the Nun at the beginning of the world*

*Principal place of worship Memphis (Lower Egypt)*

*Representation: a bearded man wearing a composite crown of the horns of a ram, a solar disc and two feathers*

In the Egyptian pantheon, several entities embody the earth. They are not necessarily deities in their own right; sometimes they are just "personifications" which symbolize an element of the cosmos or nature, a city, a necropolis, a marvelous site, or even a notion. When they concern the earth, these deities are always related to a particular aspect of this element: they sometimes recall the main function of earth which, as fertile ground, is intended to provide the organized world with vegetation or food; they also sometimes symbolize a facet of the earth, precisely determined in time or space.

The best known of these personifications is sprung from the Heliopolitan cosmogony: it is ***Geb***, the son of ***Shu*** and ***Tefenet***. He embodies the earth's hills and mountains, and the wealth the ground contains. He also watches over everything that is part of it: the minerals, animals and vegetation, but also the deceased and powers that live underground. Then there is ***Pega*** who probably represents the earth's surface. The deity ***Aker***, for his part, embodies the depths of the earth and especially the place where the deceased rest, and where the sun regenerates every day. He is depicted as a strip of earth with a human head on each extremity, and is placed at the entrance of hell to control the continuous comings and goings of the deceased, to whom he can appear both threatening and benevolent.

***Tanen*** also belongs to this group of deities. His name literally means *"the rising Land,"* and he embodies the bowels of the earth, and the Primeval Mound, the first lands that emerged from the ***Nun*** before the creation. According to some traditions, he is also the protector of the roads the god ***Re'*** uses during his nocturnal journey. It is his job to make sure there are no obstacles that could disturb the progress of the solar boat.

***Tanen*** comes from **Memphis** where, for a time, he is considered as a demiurge. He is depicted as a man wearing a long fake beard and a composite crown with the horns of a ram, a solar disc and two feathers. Here, just as in the other cosmogonic tales, the story of the world starts with ***Nun***, the primeval and inert watery abyss that symbolizes nothingness. ***Nun*** contains within itself an unconscious power that slowly awakens and grows into life under the aspect of a hill of earth that emerges from the primeval waters: this power is called ***Tanen*** and symbolizes the initial mound the world will settle on. After the 18th Dynasty, ***Ptah***, who also comes from **Memphis**, assimilates all the gods surrounding him. Under the name of ***Ptah-Sokar***, he acquires the abilities of ***Sokar***, patron of craftsmen and funerary god of the Memphite necropolis; afterwards, under the name of ***Ptah-Sokar-Osiris***, he completes his funerary duty by adopting the personality of ***Osiris***, the great god of the Underworld and of the deceased; and at last, under the name of ***Ptah-Tanen***, he becomes the creative god of **Memphis**.

Unfortunately, our knowledge of the Memphite cosmogony is very limited. There is only one document that alludes to the creation of the world by the god ***Ptah:*** it is a late stela that dates back to the reign of *Shabaqo,* a pharaoh of the 25th Dynasty. If one is to believe the text of the introduction, it is the copy of an older papyrus. Of course, no one knows whether the original text has been completely changed, or simply altered, into a tale where ***Ptah*** appears as a universal god. The stela is also quite damaged; it has many blanks, which prevent us from always understanding the religious subtleties that the priest may have introduced.

However, in spite of these doubts, it seems that in this tradition ***Tanen*** represents only one of the many facets of ***Ptah*** who, to organize his creation, borrows some aspects of the personality of deities from other cosmogonies. As a creative god, ***Ptah*** appears as well under the name of ***Ptah***, ***Tanen*** or ***Ptah-Tanen***. For instance, in the passage describing the city of **Memphis**, it is said that it is the *"granary of the god **Tanen**"* and that it *"brings joy to the hearts of the gods who are in the temple of **Ptah**."* Later on, to relate the arrival of ***Osiris*** at **Memphis**, it is written that he *"entered the palace and became friends with the gods and **Ptah-Tanen**, the master of years."*

# *Tefenet*

Tefenet 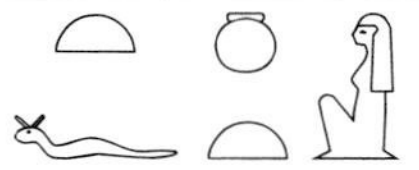

*Daughter of Re'-Atum-Khepri, the sun*

*Sister and wife of Shu, the breath of life*

*Mother of Geb, the earth, and Nut, the sky*

*Deity incarnating heat and the order of the cosmos; she sometimes has the personality of the lioness and dangerous goddess*

*Representation: a lioness or a woman with the head of a lioness*

In the Heliopolitan tradition, ***Tefenet*** is the daughter of ***Re'***, the creative god. With her brother ***Shu***, she forms the first divine couple. Because of their duties within the universe, they are complementary and inseparable. ***Tefenet*** personifies the cosmic order; ***Shu*** symbolizes life. ***Tefenet*** brings heat; ***Shu*** gives light. Both are emanations of their father, and they ensure the lighting up of the sun simply by their presence. This is clearly told in the cosmogonic documents which say, when talking of the demiurge, that *"from one, he became three"*. ***Re'*** cannot exist without his children, who are thus the original principles which allow their father to manifest himself in the created world.

Apart from her cosmic duties, ***Tefenet*** very often adopts the personality of furious deities such as the lioness ***Sakhmet***. She personifies the solar eye and certain legends describe her fearsome character and whimsical temper, as for instance in the wonderful myth about the "**Lioness of Nubia**," which goes back to the Greco-Roman period. The story is set in a time when the gods still lived on earth. ***Tefenet***, it is said, decided, of her own free will, to go into exile in the southern part of Egypt, in the country of **Nubia**. Then, she was called "the Fearful One," because, having adopted the aspects of a lioness, she wandered through the desert in search of flesh and blood. Lightning flashed from her eyes, and flames poured out her mouth. She struck terror into every heart and no one dared to approach her for fear of being devoured. But far away in **Heliopolis**, ***Re'*** was melancholy, for he wanted to see his daughter again. One day he decided to have her searched for. The divine assembly not being very enthusiastic about it, ***Re'*** summoned ***Shu*** and ***Thoth*** to convince them to go to look for ***Tefenet*** in **Nubia**. He thought that ***Shu***, being ***Tefenet***'s brother, couldn't but suffer from this long separation. He also formed with his sister the couple of "lions of the horizon" that was supposed to support the sun. This function would make him able to adopt the appearance of a lion, and thus approach ***Tefenet*** with more ease. And the demiurge believed that ***Thoth*** being Master of the divine scriptures and sacred words, would be able to persuade her to come back to her home country.

The tale takes us afterwards to **Nubia**, where our two companions finally find ***Tefenet***, and discover that she has become an enraged deity. As they cannot approach her, they turn into two little monkeys, little animals too insignificant to bother the dreadful lioness. And ***Thoth*** starts talking to her, using all his power of persuasion and his spirit to urge ***Tefenet*** to come back to the Valley of the Nile; over there, he tells her, are abundance and comfort. If she agreed to follow them to **Heliopolis**, sanctuaries would be built, festivities celebrated for her return, and she would be honored throughout the country. He flatters her, explains to her how dazzling she is: *"Your eyes are more beautiful than the sky when it is pure of clouds."* He tells her fables and moral stories. Little by little, the goddess is captivated by such a wonderful speech, and in the end, she decides to go back home with her two friends. On the way back, ***Thoth*** continues to charm her to quiet her violence he knows is latent. ***Shu***, for his part, is so happy to have found his sister again, that he just dances around her. When they arrive at the doors of Egypt, they plunge the goddess into the freezing waters of the **Abaton** to calm her aggressiveness. She comes out of this forced bath in the peaceful demeanor of the goddess ***Hathor***, definitely free of her fearful aspects. The journey which takes her to her father in **Heliopolis** lasts nine days. On both sides of the river, ***Tefenet***, daughter of ***Re'***, is glorified, and she is welcomed with offerings and dances.

This legend stresses the journey of the sun and the cyclical return of the floods. The isolation of ***Tefenet*** in **Nubia**, under the aspect of the "Fearful One", symbolizes the period of drought, whereas her return to Egypt, under the aspect of the peaceful ***Hathor***, coincides with the rising of the waters of the Nile, and thus the flood. So the daughter of the sun is closely related to the blessing of the inundation, upon which the survival of the Egyptian people depends; thus theology confirms the omnipotence of the sun.

## From Thoth the ibis...

*Thoth can appear under two distinct iconographies according to which context he is in: generally, Thoth the ibis is the divine book-keeper, whereas Thoth the baboon is the patron of scribes. Of course, all this is theoretical. In fact, across the centuries, the two pictures of the god of scriptures finally merge, and both images are indifferently used by the artist. This bronze statuette shows Thoth with the head of an ibis, in the attitude of a man apparently walking; he carries a small tabernacle which contains the wedjat eye. This representation is a reference to one of the multiple episodes of the Osirian myth, which tells how Seth, after having murdered his brother, fights Horus with the idea of claiming the earthly kingdom. In one of the struggles between the two of them, Seth manages to take the eye of his enemy, which Thoth restores before taking it back to Re', the solar god of Heliopolis.*

Late Period.

*Next pages*

## ... to Thoth the baboon

*Many documents show this scene of the weighing of the heart. However, the analysis of these different images show that there is no definite representation of this scene. The divinities appear and disappear according to the will of the artist, even if some of them should not be absent in such an event. This is true for Osiris, who presides over the funerary judgment, or for Anubis who checks the weighing. This is also true for the "Great Eater" who must devour the heart of the deceased in case of an unfavorable judgment. In the Neferubenef papyrus, all three of them are absent. Ma'at, the goddess of justice, is largely present with her ostrich feather. As for Thoth, the baboon perched on the pedestal, he passively contemplates the weighing.*

New Kingdom.

# *Thoth*

Thoth 

*Deity with many activities, god of the moon, god of scriptures and sciences, messenger and recorder of the gods, master of knowledge, patron of scribes*

*Principal place of worship: Hermopolis (Central Egypt)*

*Representation: man with the head of an ibis or a baboon*

***Thoth*** is the ibis god who comes from the **nome** of **Hermopolis**, in Central Egypt. He very soon becomes one of the great gods of the Egyptian pantheon, as the faithful lieutenant of the king of gods. He was given this rank by the demiurge himself as a token for his wisdom and his competence. The birth of ***Thoth*** is still mysterious: according to different traditions, he would be born from the skull of ***Seth*** or from the heart of the creator in a moment of sadness. In any case, his success and his celebrity are due to his indisputable qualities rather than to his modest origin. For ***Thoth*** is hardworking. His responsibilities in the administration of the world are many. He becomes the instrument that allows the [redacted] to materialize his creation. He is the master of all sciences, he knows and understands everything. Because he is the holder of all knowledge, it is up to him to spread it. This is why he invented a tool that made the transmission of the sciences possible through thousands of years: the art of writing. He is the undisputed master of the "divine words," the hieroglyphs; he is the author of everything written, and the patron of the scribes. It is believed that men inherited everything from ***Thoth***, and that this sum of knowledge was transmitted to them through books and scriptures that were deliberately left to them by the god in the sanctuaries.

However, ***Thoth*** is so acutely aware of his intellectual superiority that he becomes tiresome, presumptuous and pompous. He likes highly finished speeches, he uses complicated words and has an affected intonation: he loves the sound of his own voice. Inevitably, he irritates. The other deities although greatly respecting his unlimited science, do not hesitate to tell him so. Here is a little anecdote which perfectly illustrates this irritation. The goddess ***Isis***, who is hiding from ***Seth***, goes to find refuge in the marshes of **Chemnis** with her son. But one evening, she discovers that little ***Horus*** is very sick. Not knowing what the origin of the sickness is, she asks ***Re'*** to help her. He sends ***Thoth*** to her, for his talents as a magician are well-known. He looks at the child, debates, talks it over, speaks about subjects that have nothing to do with it. Angered, ***Isis*** orders him to shut up and says: *"**Thoth**, how wise is your heart, but how slow are your decisions."*

***Thoth***, as undisputed master of all knowledge, has competencies in many fields. He is the god of mathematics and as such is a wonderful calculator. It is he on his own who fixed the limits of the nomes and the borders of the countries: he *"created the regulation of the Double Land and the organization of the provinces."* It is said too that he built the sanctuaries of the gods, for he alone knows how to draw plans and how to correctly orient the buildings. All sciences are under his control and need his patronage; he is patron of scribes, doctors, astronomers, magicians and architects. Apart from his terrestrial duties, ***Thoth*** has celestial functions. According to the will of the demiurge, he is the moon god. A myth recalls how he inherited this role. The story starts as ***Re'***, tired of the quarrels and incessant revolts of men, decides to leave the earth to settle in the celestial heights. This departure upsets the organization of time, since from then on, the sun illuminates the earth during the day, disappears at night to light the underground world, and reappears only at dawn. The night is thus completely deprived of light and the stars do not give enough luminosity. So ***Thoth***, the moon, takes the place of the sun while it goes for its nightly journey. It is ***Re'*** himself who gives this duty to ***Thoth:*** *"You shall be in my place, my substitute. You shall be called **Thoth**, the substitute of **Re'**. I make it so that your beauty and your light encircle the two skies. In that manner, the moon of **Thoth** came into existence."* This moon duty makes him the master of stars and time. He is the inventor of the calendar, since through his action, he differentiates the days, months, seasons and years.

Last but not least, he plays his part in the next world. He is the divine book-keeper and messenger of the funerary gods. During the weighing of the heart, it is he who writes down the verdict of the goddess ***Ma'at*** on the sacred tablets. It is also he who introduces the deceased into the judgment hall and takes him to ***Osiris***. An excerpt of the Chapter 125 of the "**Book of the Dead**" recapitulates the role of ***Thoth***. Here, the deceased comes to the door of the room where the deities of the netherworld are sitting. He tries to go in, but he is intercepted by ***Thoth***:

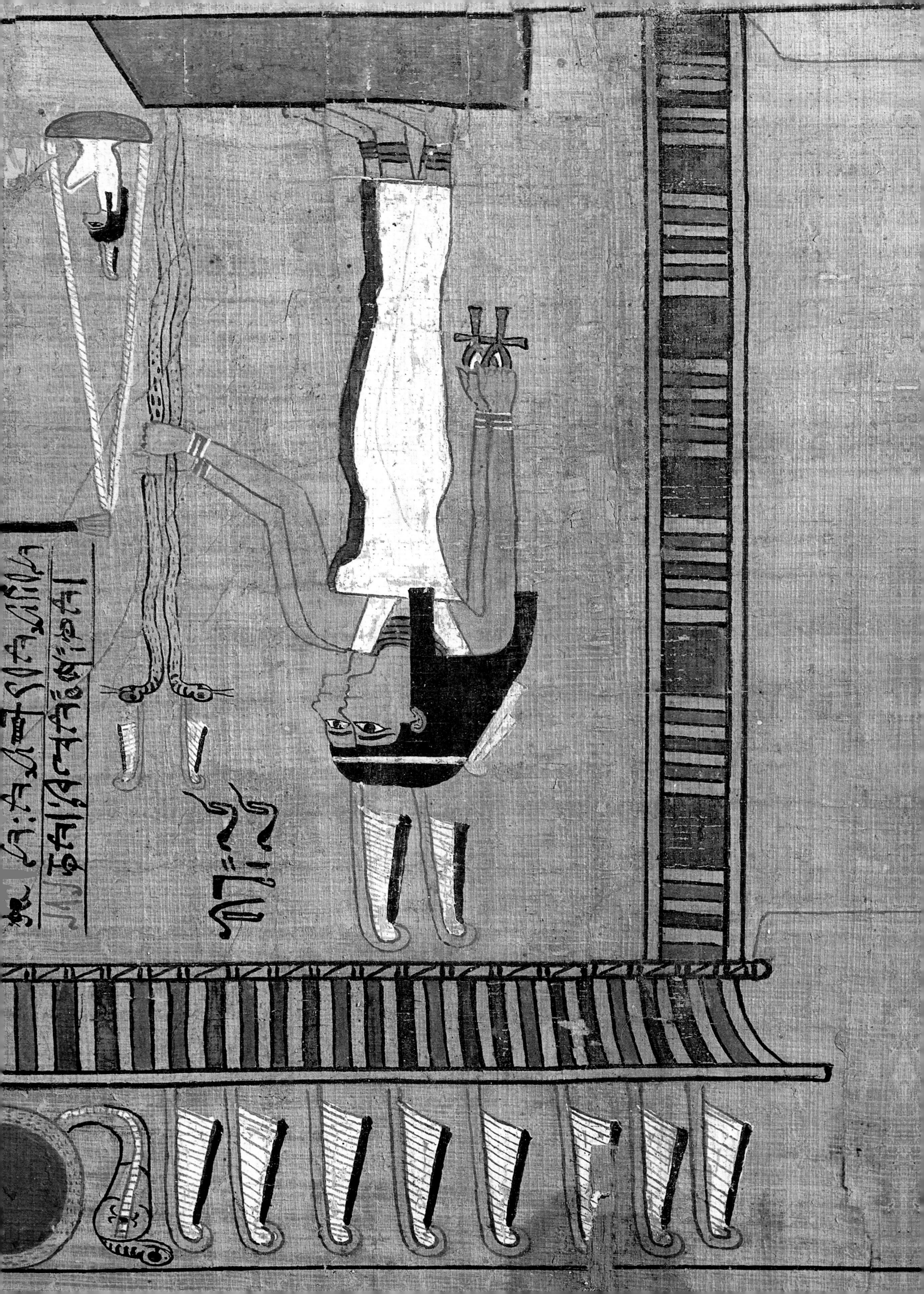

*"The voice of **Thoth**, who is invisible, says then:*
*- Tell me first, why do you come here?*
*- I come here to be announced.*
*- What is your condition? What kind of a man are you?*
*- I am cleaned of all sin and I am a stranger to the faults of men who obey on the spur of the moment: I am not one of them!*
*- I shall usher you to the divinity if you tell me this: what is the name of the deity who is protected by a sky of fire, who is surrounded by a wall of snake goddesses, who rests on the surface of running waters?*
*- It is **Osiris**.*
*- Cross the threshold! In truth I can give your name!"*

All the mythological tales and legends stage deities in a world organized in the same fashion as the world of men. The Universal Master reigns at the head of the divine administration, just as the Pharaoh does on earth. He is assisted by ***Thoth***, the divine bookkeeper, who has the same competence as the vizier of the Pharaonic government. Both act as the right hand of their master and control the proper working of the administration. In fact, the Universal Master especially interferes in times of serious crisis, such as when there is a conflict between several gods. Otherwise, it is ***Thoth*** who manages the thousand worries of everyday life. Within the divine community, he knows how to be respected by the other gods, because they value his abilities. ***Thoth*** constantly appears next to the king of gods. Very often he acts as his loyal counselor. The Universal Master never hesitates to refer to him when he has a problem, and ***Thoth*** utters his opinion, gives counsels lavishly, and offers solutions.

The divine community is subject to a certain number of laws dictated by the creator (the Universal Master) at the beginning of time. When a conflict cannot be solved by the simple observance of the established rules, the gods gather in an unusual assembly to try to solve the problems. After the debate and discussions, which can sometimes last for years, the decision is made, and it is published by ***Thoth*** who also has the charge of having it applied. No resolution can be effective if it has not been certified and registered by ***Thoth***, who makes sure that everybody has knowledge of it. These divine ordinances can apply to all kinds of subjects: they may regulate a particular aspect of everyday life, pass a sentence or assess a new law.

**Taweret followed by Anukis**

*No other deity of the Egyptian pantheon is as good-natured as Taweret, the protector of women and children. Whatever her iconography, she always appears as a familiar and sympathetic being: she can either be, as here in the tomb of Nekhtamun, a hippopotamus with the head of a woman, or she can be just a hippopotamus. She walks on her hind legs, with her stomach pushed out, evoking a pregnant woman; Taweret has to protect during pregnancy, help during the delivery and assist during nursing. Behind her is Anukis, the child goddess of the Elephantine triad, who is recognizable by her tall crown of feathers.*

Tomb 355 of Nekhtamun, Deir el-Medina, New Kingdom, West Thebes, Upper Egypt.

# *Taweret*

Taweret 

Protector of homes, women and children

Principal place of worship: no special or particular temple, but in each home

Representation: a women with a hybrid body

The goddess ***Taweret*** belongs, just as the dwarf ***Bes***, to the home and to family life. Her most faithful admirers are amongst the people who consider her to be the guardian of homes and families. Her main role is to protect women and their children. She specially guarantees female fertility, assures easy births and cares for the nursing of the newborn children. She is called "the White One," "the Big One" or "the Harem".

She is said to help women in childbirth, whether goddesses, queens or ordinary women; that is why her help is necessary during pregnancy and delivery. To be sure of her permanent protection, women have to wear an amulet bearing her effigy or to possess in their houses a statuette that reminds them of her presence at their sides. ***Taweret*** has a very specific iconography. She has a hybrid body: half hippopotamus, and half crocodile, with human hands and lion feet. She stands on her rear legs: and close to her is the magic knot, symbol of protection. This particular representation is a reminder of her role towards women: her prominent belly and heavy breasts give a reassuring image of a pregnant woman.

Excavations made in dwelling areas have brought to light strange objects which were, it seems, supposed to create abundant milk for young mothers. They are hollow figurines made out of terracotta or crockery, which represent the goddess ***Taweret***. One of her breasts, proudly raised as a sign of nursing, is pierced with a hole and has a small cork. It is said that, on the day of the childbirth, the statuette was filled with milk, and the cork was taken out: the milk dripped slowly out, and by magic it prevented the owner of the object from being without milk. Votive statuettes have been also found with a similar appearance; but they probably had a very different use. For still unknown reasons, pieces of cloth having belonged to pregnant women were kept within these statuettes.

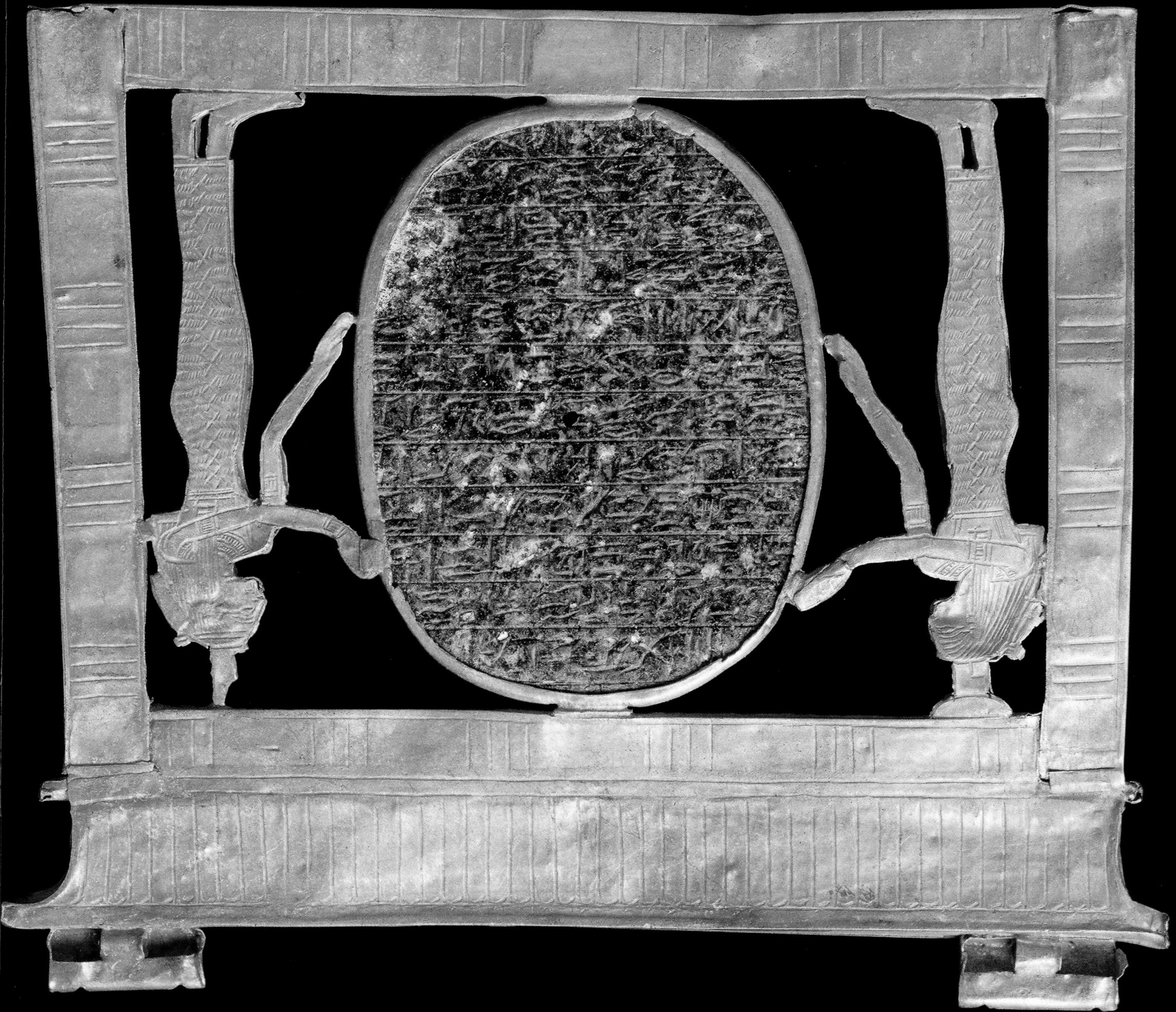

# MAP OF EGYPT

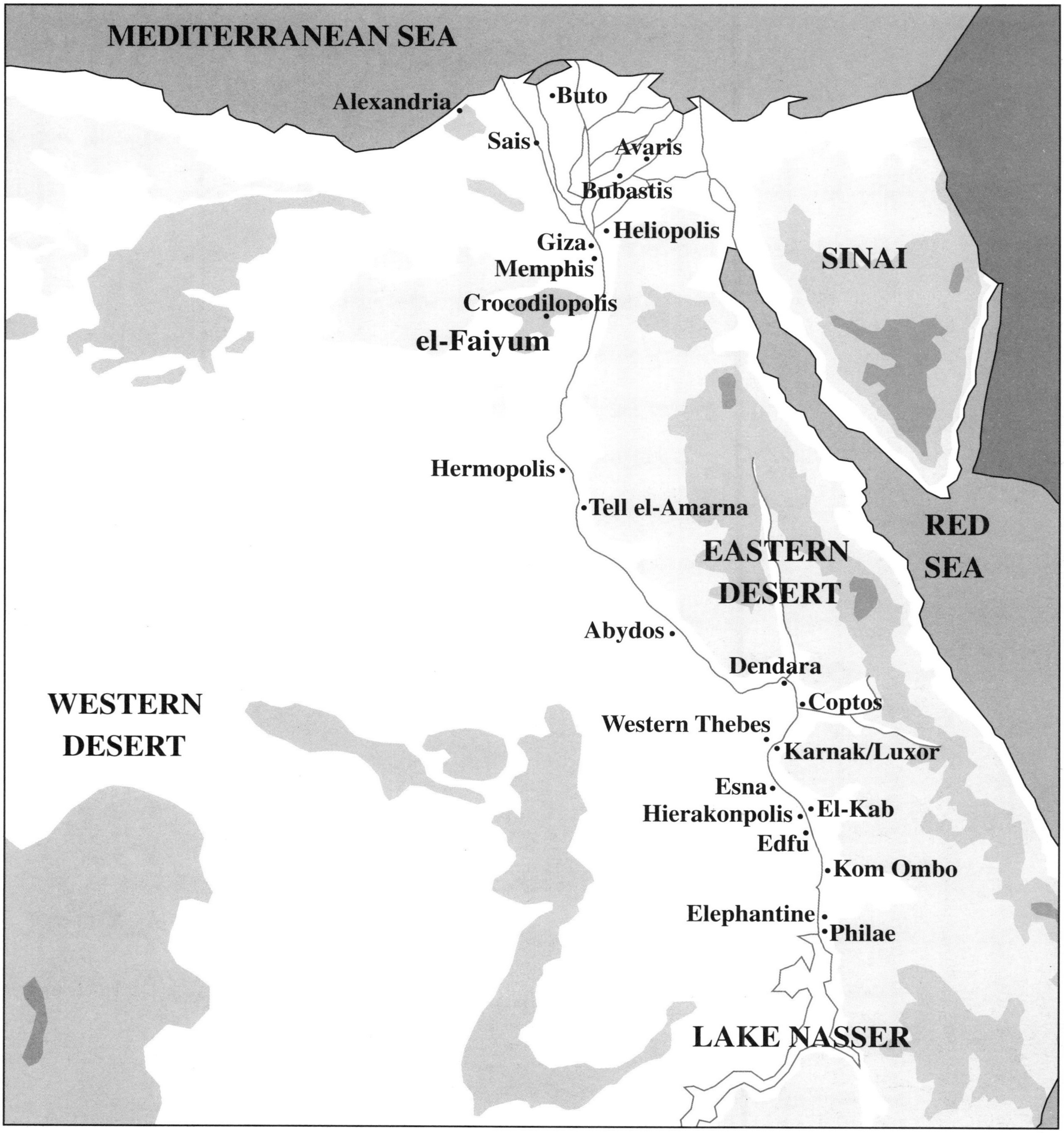
MEDITERRANEAN SEA
Alexandria
•Buto
Sais•
Avaris
Bubastis
•Heliopolis
Giza•
Memphis
Crocodilopolis
el-Faiyum
SINAI
Hermopolis •
•Tell el-Amarna
EASTERN
DESERT
RED
SEA
Abydos •
Dendara
•Coptos
WESTERN
DESERT
Western Thebes
•Karnak/Luxor
Esna•
Hierakonpolis •
•El-Kab
Edfu
•Kom Ombo
Elephantine •
•Philae
LAKE NASSER

# A FEW GODS

## *Iconography and representations*

***Amun***

***Anubis***

***Apis***

***Apophis***

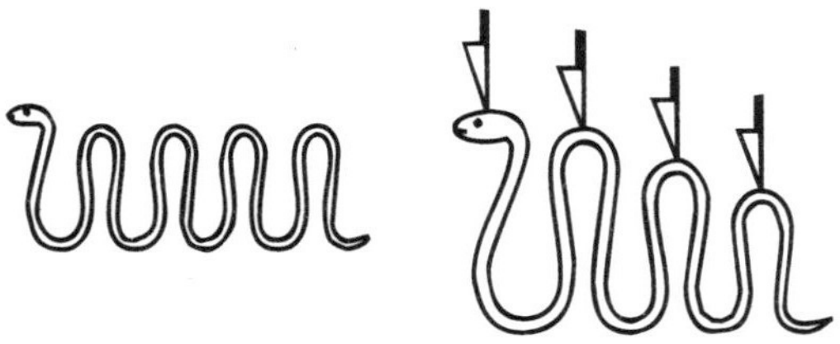

***Aten***

***Atum***

***Bes***

***Ha'py***

***Harakhty***

***Horus***

***Khepri***

***Khnum***

***Khons***

***Min***

***Montu***

***Nefertem***

***Osiris***

***Ptah***

***Re'***

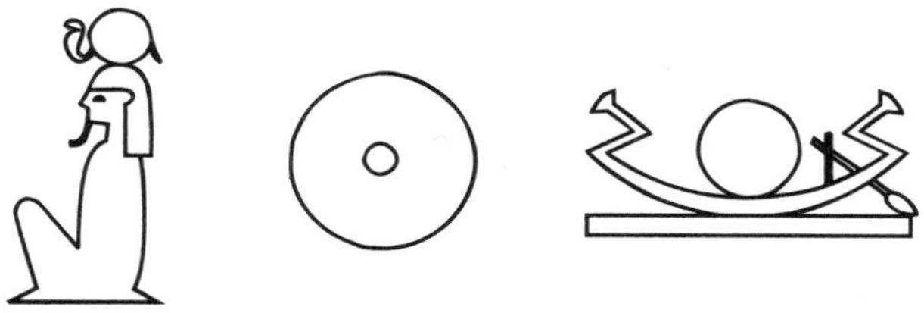

***Seth***

***Shu***

***Sobek***

***Sokar***

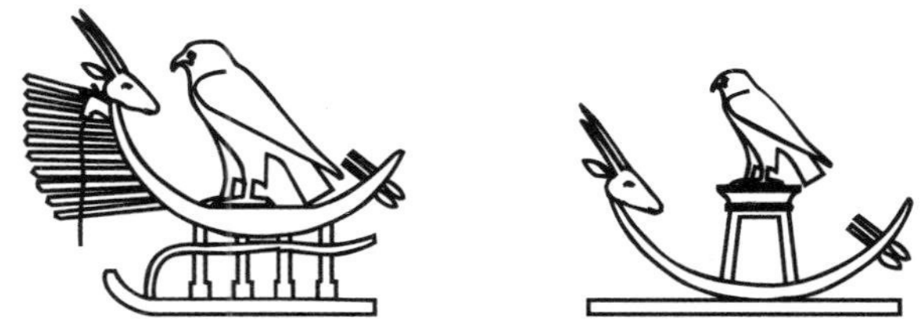

***Sopd***

***Thoth***

***Wepwawet***

# A FEW GODDESSES

## *Iconography and representations*

***Bastet***

***Hathor***
***(woman)***

***Hathor***
***(cow)***

***Heqet***

***Isis***

***Isis***
***(with Nephthys)***

***Isis***
***(with Osiris and Horus)***

***Isis***
***(with Harpokrates)***

***Ma'at***

***Mut***

***Neith***

***Neith***
***(as the cow Ihet carrying Re')***

***Nekhbet***

***Nekhbet (with Wadjit)***

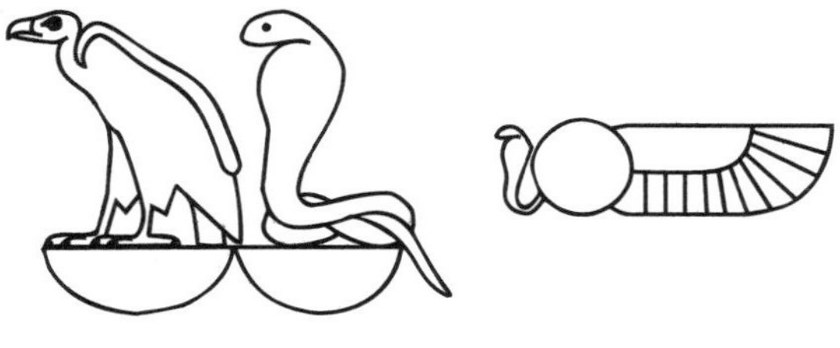

***Nephthys***

***Nut***

***Nut (with the sun)***

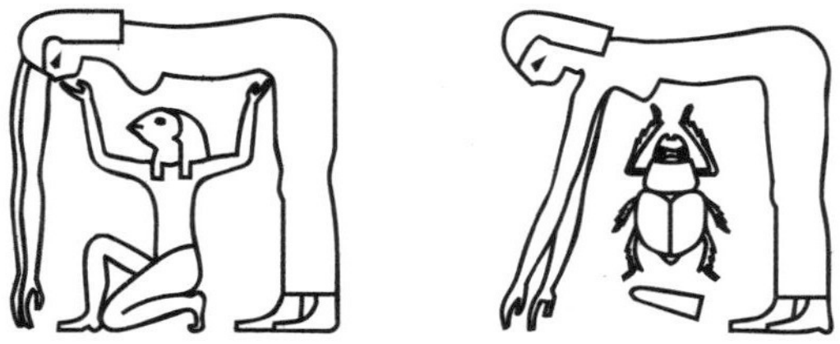

***Sakhmet***

***Satis***

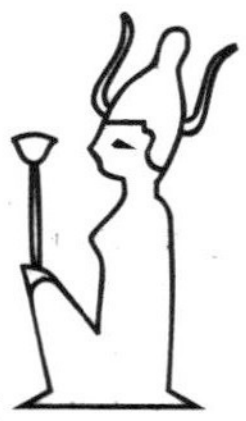

***Serket***

***Seshat***

***Sopdet***

***Taweret***

***Tefenet***

***Tefenet (with Shu)***

***Wadjit***

# SYMBOLS

## Amulets, scepters and crowns

***ankh cross***

symbol of life and vital breath

***chen sign***

symbol of *"what the sun surrounds"*: the universe

***djed pillar***

symbol of duration and stability

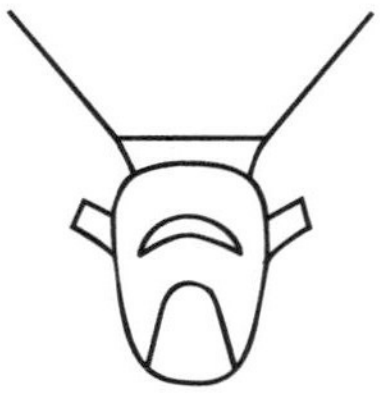

***ib heart***

symbol of intelligence and consciousness

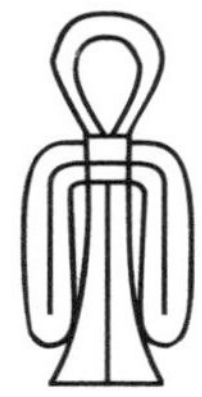

***magic girdle (girdle of Isis)***

guarantees protection in all circumstances

***sistrum of Hathor***

symbol of music, festivals and sacred rites

***kheper dung beetle***

symbol of existence

***stem of papyrus***

imparts fertility, fecundity and vigor

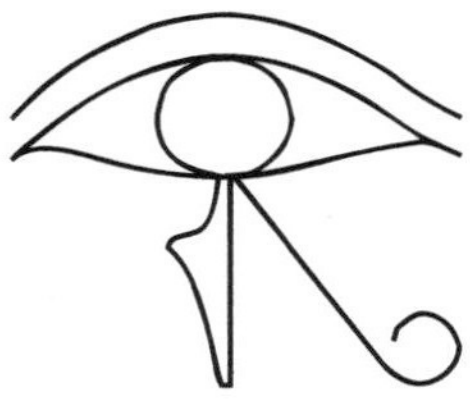

***wedjat eye (eye of Horus)***

symbol of health, integrity and abundance

***symbol of gold***

symbolizes the inalterability of the divine body

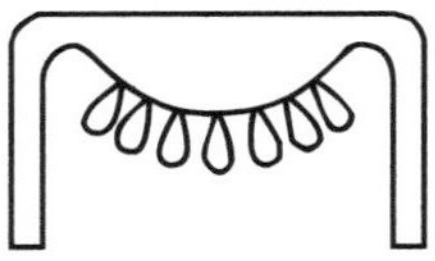

***heka scepter (cross)***

generally held by ***Osiris*** and Pharaoh

***flagellum (flail)***

generally held by ***Osiris*** and Pharaoh

***was scepter (with the head of a dog)***

held by gods and goddesses

***double feather (arrow) with emblem***

the Orient and the Eastern countries

***feather on a mast***

the Occident and the Western countries

***sema-tawi***

symbol of the union of the two kingdoms of Egypt

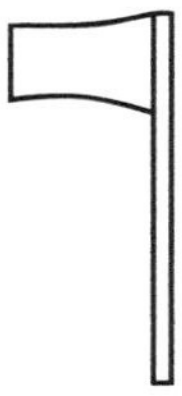

***banner***

symbol of the concept of divinity

***cartouche***

symbolizes the universal reign of Pharaoh

***feather of Ma'at***

symbol of truth and justice

***obelisk***

symbolizes a ray of sun, evoking the solar cult

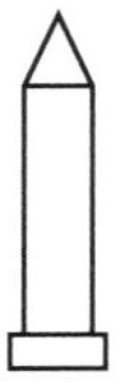

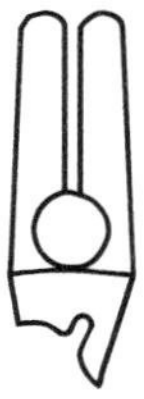

***Amun***

upside down mortar crowned with two feathers and the solar disc

***Bes***

crown with four high feathers

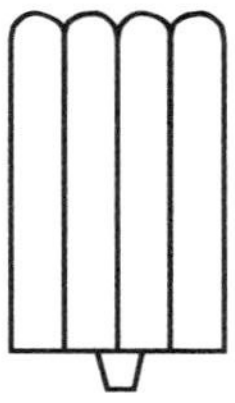

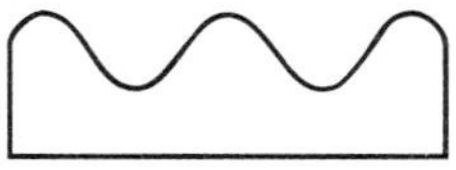

***Ha***

head crowned with the emblem of foreign countries and deserts

***Ha'py***

head crowned with a papyrus bouquet

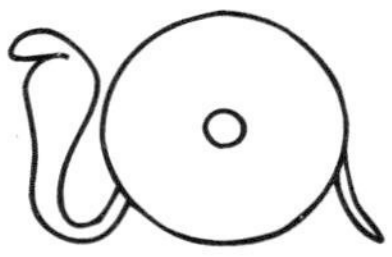

***Harakhty***

head crowned with a cobra and the solar disc

***Hathor***

two horns of a cow surrounding the solar disc

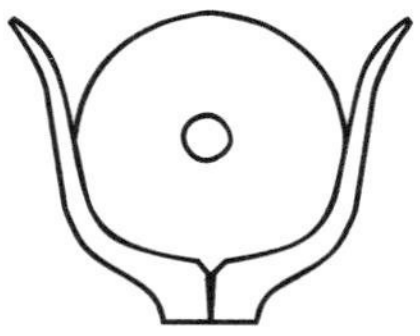

***Horus***

crown of Upper and Lower Egypt (called **pschent**)

***Isis***

head crowned with a throne (symbol of ***Isis***)

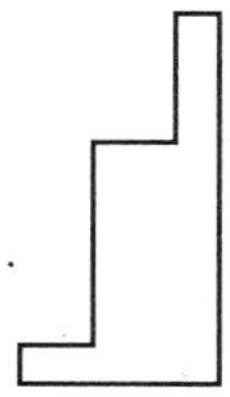

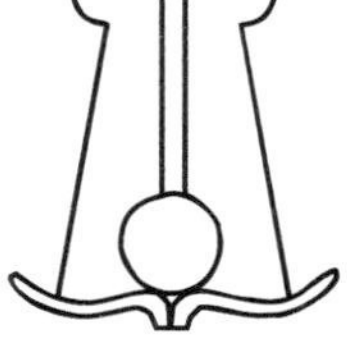

***Khnum***

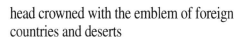

crown of two horns of a ram upholding two feathers and the solar disc

***Khons***

head crowned with the solar and lunar discs

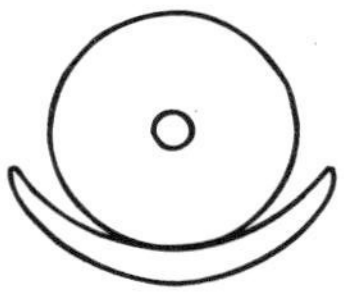

***Ma'at***

head crowned with an ostrich feather

***Min***

crown with two high feathers (a variant of ***Amun***'s crown)

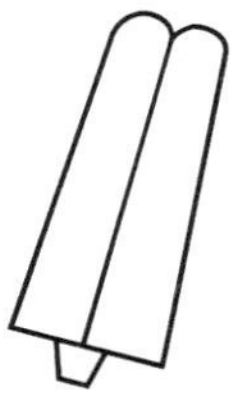

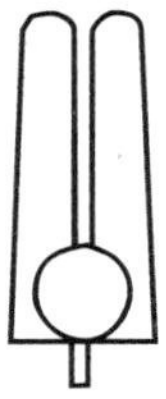

***Montu***

crown with two high feathers and the solar disc (a variant of ***Amun***'s crown)

***Nefertem***

head crowned with a lotus flower

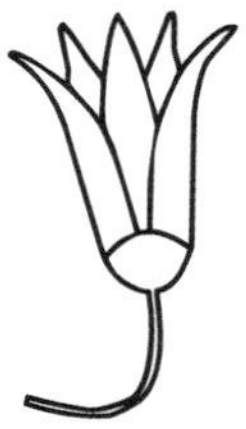

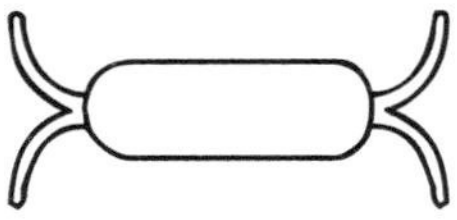

***Neith***

head crowned with two bows tied in a sheath (symbol of ***Neith***)

***Nekhbet***

white crown of Upper Egypt

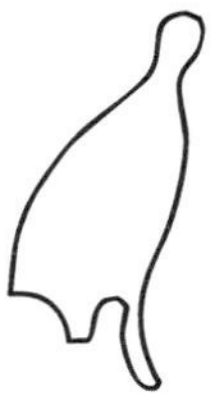

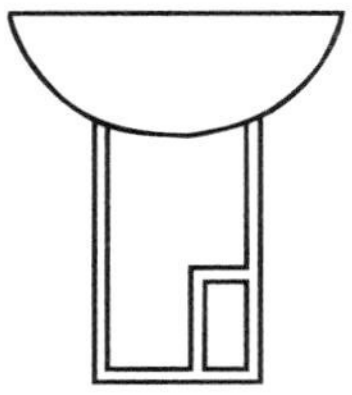

***Nephthys***

head crowned with a basket and the plan of a house (symbol of ***Nephthys***)

***Osiris***

white crown of Upper Egypt flanked with two feathers (called **atef** crown)

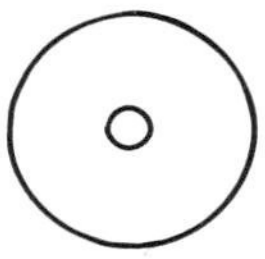

***Re'***

head crowned with the solar disc

***Serket***

head crowned with the corpse of a scorpion

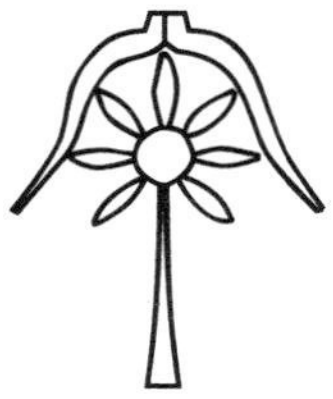

***Seshat***

rosette on a pole with seven branches crowned with two overturned horns (symbol of ***Séshat***)

***Sobek***

ram's horn crown with two feathers, the solar disc and two cobras

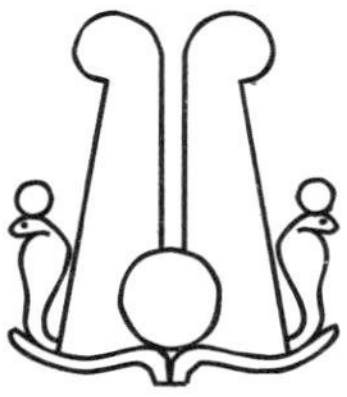

***Sopdet***

head crowned with a star (symbol of ***Sopdet***)

***Wadjit***

red crown of Lower Egypt

# LEXICON OF DIVINITIES

***Aker*** - He is an old personification of earth and of the underworld depicted either as a double sphinx or as a strip of earth with a human head on each extremity. ***Aker*** is placed at the entrance of hell to control the incessant comings and goings of the deceased, to whom he appears at the same time threatening and benevolent.

***Amaunet*** - Her name means *"the One that cannot be seen,"* or the *"Hidden One."* She forms with **Amun** one of the four primeval couples who preceded the creation of the world in the cosmogony of **Hermopolis**. In this tradition, **Amun** and **Amaunet** are not deities but personifications of emptiness or of spatial indefiniteness.

***Amun*** - He originally comes from **Thebes**, but becomes the national and dynastic god from the Middle Kingdom on. His main place of worship is in **Thebes** (**Luxor** and **Karnak**) where he is venerated with the goddess **Mut** and the god son **Khons**.

***Anubis*** - This funerary god, depicted as a black jackal or as a man with the head of a jackal, is supposed to be the inventor of mummification and, therefore, makes sure the embalming ceremonies are properly conducted. He is, in a wider sense, the protector of the necropolis.

***Anukis*** - She is the infant goddess of the **Elephantine** triad. With the god ***Khnum*** and the goddess ***Satis***, she is guardian of the sources of the Nile and patroness of the cataract. She is depicted as a woman wearing a crown of feathers. Sometimes she is followed by a gazelle, traditionally associated with the Nile.

***Apis*** - The sacred bull from **Memphis** is considered to be the representative of ***Ptah*** on earth. He is sometimes associated with ***Osiris*** and ***Re***'; in this case, he adopts funerary and solar characteristics. The sacred bulls are buried in particular necropolises called **Serapeums**.

***Apophis*** - He is a giant, malevolent snake who represents all the destructive forces and powers of chaos. He is the symbol of evil.

***Aten*** - He is the solar disc above all. He appears as early as the Old Kingdom period, but it is only under the 18th dynasty that pharaoh *Akhenaten* elevates him as the only dynastic god.

***Atum*** - He is one of the three forms of the creative and solar god of **Heliopolis**. ***Atum*** represents the setting sun, whereas ***Re***' and ***Khepri*** are the moon and rising sun.

***Bastet*** - This cat goddess, worshipped in the Delta at **Bubastis**, is the incarnation of the peaceful aspects of the dangerous goddesses. Her name is symbol of joy and goodness, which is why her cult is so popular.

***Bes*** - He is a domestic spirit, very popular in every household, considered to be the protector of children and women. His grotesque dances and horrible grimaces are supposed to drive out the evil spirits and hostile forces that haunt houses.

***Four Sons of Horus*** - They are the "Masters of the Cardinal Points", and protectors of the **canopic jars** of the deceased: ***Imset*** the genie of the South, ***Duamutef*** the genie of the East, ***Hapy*** the genie of the North and ***Qebehsenuf*** the genie of the West.

***Geb*** - He represents the earth and all the riches that are in the soil. With ***Nut***, ***Geb*** forms the second divine couple of the great Heliopolitan Ennead.

***Ha'py*** - He represents the inundation and the flood of the Nile, which guarantee the fertility of cultivated fields. As a symbol of plenty, ***Ha'py*** is depicted as an androgynous deity, sometimes female and sometimes male, with hanging breasts.

***Harakhty*** - *"**Horus** of the Horizon"* is one of the forms of the creative and solar god from **Heliopolis**.

***Harmakhis*** - *"**Horus** on the Horizon"* is a solar deity represented by the Sphinx of **Giza**.

***Haroeris*** - *"**Horus** the Great"* is the falcon god from **Kom-Ombo**, who fights against the enemies of ***Re***'. In certain traditions, he is related to the cosmogony of **Heliopolis**, where he is *"**Horus** the Elder,"* one of the five children of ***Geb*** and ***Nut***.

***Harpokrates*** - *"**Horus** the Child"* is the designation for ***Horus*** as child of ***Isis*** and ***Osiris***. Contrary to ***Horus,*** who is intended to grow up, ***Harpokrates*** is meant to stay forever as a child and be the symbol of childhood.

***Hathor*** - She is one of the most popular goddesses of the Egyptian pantheon. She has all kinds of duties: she is goddess of beauty, love and joy, patroness of the Theban necropolis, celestial deity, mistress of the foreign lands, nurse of the royal child… She became so popular over the years that she acquired the personalities of other feminine deities, such as ***Isis***.

***Heqet*** - This goddess with a frog's head, is associated, in **Antinoe**, with the potter and creative god, ***Khnum***. When there is a union between a god and a royal wife, a theogamy, so as to give birth to a future king, she helps her divine husband shape the body of the infant.

***Horus*** - He is the son of ***Isis*** and ***Osiris***, who inherits from his grandfather, the god ***Geb***, the kingdom of earth. ***Horus*** is the main dynastic god, and the pharaohs are under his direct protection. He is also a solar and a celestial god; as such, he is associated with the goddess ***Hathor*** who is his wife.

***Hurun*** - This Canaanite deity is a solar god assimilated with ***Harmakhis*** and incarnated by the Sphinx of **Giza**.

***Isis*** - She is wife and sister of ***Osiris***, mother of ***Horus***, and she has a very strong personality that confers many roles on her: protector of women and children, great magician, protector of the mummy of the deceased, universal goddess…

***Khentimentiu*** - As most of the canine gods, this jackal deity has funerary functions. In the beginning, he is the god of the dead and protector of the **Abydos**'s necropolis but, towards the end of the Old Kingdom, ***Osiris*** absorbs his personality and he only appears as a simple epithet of the great god of the dead.

***Khepri*** - He is the god honored in **Heliopolis** under the form of a dung beetle. He symbolizes the rising sun which is reborn every morning; with ***Atum***, the setting sun, and ***Re'***, the sun at noon, he is considered to be the creative god.

***Khnum*** - This god with a ram's head has several places of worship: in **Elephantine** as the god of the cataract and the guardian of the sources of the Nile, in triad with ***Satis*** and ***Anukis***; in **Esna**, he is the creative god. It is told that, on his potter's wheel, he has fashioned gods, men and objects.

***Khons*** - He is the" Wanderer" or the "Traveler," and is in direct relation with the moon. In the 18th dynasty, he is associated with the god ***Amun*** and the goddess ***Mut*** as the son god of the Theban triad.

***Ma'at*** - She symbolizes truth and justice. On earth, she guarantees cosmic balance and universal order. In the afterworld, she determines the weight of the sins of the deceased. Men and gods have to obey her rule and respect what she represents.

***Min*** - He is the god of fertility associated, in this role, with ***Amun***, the god of the Kingdom. He is worshipped in **Coptos** and ***Akhmim*** as protector of the caravans and patron of the oriental desert tracks.

***Mnevis*** - The sacred bull of **Heliopolis**, established under the name of **Mnevis**, appears at the beginning of the New Kingdom as a manifestation of the solar god.

***Montu*** - He is a falcon god from **Thebes**, who incarnates the irresistible force of war.

***Mut*** - In **Thebes**, this vulture goddess is the divine consort of ***Amun*** and the mother of the god ***Khons***. She sometimes adopted the features of the warrior lion goddesses as ***Sakhmet***.

***Nefertem*** - The sun emerged from this primeval lotus at the beginning of time. Several deities are associated with him: in **Memphis**, he is the son of ***Ptah*** and ***Sakhmet***, in **Bubastis** the son of the cat goddess ***Bastet*** and in **Buto** the son of the cobra goddess ***Wadjit***.

***Neith*** - She has several functions: she is the warrior goddess of the town of **Sais** and demiurge of the town of **Esna**. In the underground world, she protects the **canopic jars** of the deceased with ***Isis***, ***Nephthys*** and ***Serket***.

***Nekhbet*** - She is the vulture goddess of **El-Kab** and protector of Upper Egypt.

***Nephthys*** - She belongs to the second generation of the gods of the Heliopolitan Ennead, with ***Osiris***, ***Isis***, ***Horus the Elder*** and ***Seth***. Her role is essentially funerary, as she watches over the body of the deceased and his **canopic jars**.

***Nun*** - He is the primeval ocean that precedes creation in the cosmogonies and represents nothingness: *"before the existence of the sky, before the existence of the earth, before the existence of men, before the existence of death"* was ***Nun***.

***Nut*** - She is the representation of the celestial vault. In the Heliopolitan cosmogony, she forms with ***Geb***, the earth, the second divine couple. The day and night journey of the sun are made on her body, which is the symbol of the space through which the sun travels.

***Osiris*** - He is the god of the dead in the Egyptian pantheon, who also represents, because of his resurrection, the yearly revival of vegetation. Everyone tries to identify himself with ***Osiris*** in the afterworld, and to enter his kingdom, since it is only he who can give hope of eternal life.

***Ptah*** - At the beginning, he is the patron of goldsmiths, sculptors and craftsmen; he is considered as the inventor of technical skills. Afterwards, he becomes the creative god of **Memphis** in the triad where he is the husband of ***Sakhmet*** and the father of ***Nefertem***. In time he merges with ***Sokar*** and ***Osiris*** to form ***Ptah-Sokar-Osiris***, and with ***Tanen*** to form ***Ptah-Tanen***.

***Re'*** - He is pre-eminently the solar god, the most important deity of the Egyptian Pantheon. His main place of worship is in **Heliopolis,** but he is venerated throughout Egypt under many names: ***Re'-Harakhty, Amun-Re', Re'-Atum, Sobek-Re'***...

***Renenutet*** - This goddess is depicted as a snake or as a woman with the head of a snake, and is considered to be the mother of ***Neper***, the god of grain. She is particularly worshipped in **el-Faiyum**, where she is the goddess of the harvest.

***Sakhmet*** - She is a power of destruction, incarnating the solar eye and dangerous forces. She is depicted as a goddess with the head of a lioness. She belongs to the Memphite triad, wife of ***Ptah*** and mother of ***Nefertem***. In **Thebes**, she is assimilated with the goddess ***Mut*** as a healing goddess.

***Sarapis*** - The pharaohs of the Greek period created this god in **Alexandria** to help the interests of the new political regime. He is the protector of the ptolemaic dynasty and of the town of **Alexandria**. He also has agrarian and funerary functions, and was the healing god of the kingdom.

***Satis*** - She is both guardian of the sources of the Nile and patroness of the cataract, associated with ***Khnum*** and ***Anukis***.

***Serket*** - On earth, this scorpion goddess heals bites and stings. In the afterworld, she is a protector, with ***Isis***, ***Nephthys*** and ***Neith*** of the viscera of the deceased, which are preserved in the **canopic jars**.

***Seshat*** - She appears as the partner of ***Thoth***, and in his company is mistress of mathematics and science, and patron of writing. She is said to detain the annals of the organized world, upon which are registered the royal feats of glory and main events of royalty.

***Seth*** - This god with the head of a mythical animal has many facets, some positive and some negative. He is at the same time the protector of the sun boat, and the murderer of ***Osiris***. In the Late Period, he symbolizes "the Foreigner" and "the Invader": he is the force of evil, trouble and disorder.

***Shu*** - With ***Tefenet***, he forms the first divine couple of the Heliopolitan cosmogony. They both are born of the solar god, allowing him to reveal himself, thanks to their power. ***Shu*** is particularly the god of space and air who symbolizes the breath of life.

***Sobek*** - The crocodile god has several places of worship, the most famous ones being in the region of **el-Faiyum** and in **Kom-Ombo**. In certain cases he is the creative god, but he is most often a protector of men against wild beasts and hostile forces that live in the marshes and the waters of the Nile.

***Sokar*** - Originally, he shares the role as patron of craftsmen with ***Ptah***; he is especially protector of the blacksmiths and the metal workers. He is soon merged with ***Ptah*** under the name of ***Ptah-Sokar-Osiris***, and he becomes the funerary god of the Memphite necropolis.

***Sopd*** - This falcon god, particularly worshipped in the eastern part of the Delta, protects the oriental borders of Egypt and the roads leading to the **Sinai**.

***Sopdet*** - She embodies the star of **Sirius** and, in this context, is related to the rising waters, the flood, fertility and the beginning of the world.

***Tanen*** - He is a very ancient Egyptian god. At the beginning, he is demiurge in **Memphis** and incarnates the first mound of earth that emerged from ***Nun*** at the beginning of the world. He is soon merged with ***Ptah*** to form ***Ptah-Tanen***.

***Taweret*** - She has no particular place of worship, but is venerated in all Egyptian households as goddess protector of pregnant women and children.

***Tefenet*** - In the Heliopolitan tradition, she is the daughter of ***Re'*** and forms, with ***Shu***, the breath of life, the first divine couple. She personifies the cosmic order and heat, without which the sun cannot reveal itself. She sometimes becomes "the Fearful One" and acquires the personality of the dangerous lion goddesses.

***Thoth*** - He is sometimes depicted as an ibis and sometimes as a baboon. He has many functions and many powers: he is the moon god, the inventor of writing and science, the protector of scribes, the master of knowledge, the divine messenger and bookkeeper. In the afterworld, he is responsible for the proper weighing of hearts, and he writes down the verdict on the sacred scriptures.

***Wadjit*** - She is the cobra goddess of **Buto**, and protector of Lower Egypt.

***Wepwawet*** - *"The one who opens the roads"* is a jackal worshipped in **Asyut** as a funerary god, and in **Abydos** as a deity closely linked to ***Osiris***'s cult.

# LEXICON

***Amulets*** - These objects are little figurines serving to protect the living and the dead. Living Egyptians wear amulets as pendants, and the deceased have them placed in their linen wrappings. They are made of faience, precious or semi-precious stone, bronze, gold, silver... They either represent divinities or hieroglyphic signs full of meaning: the **djed** pillar (longevity and stability), the **ankh** cross (life), the **wedjat** eye (plenty), the **kheper** dung beetle (existence) or the **girdle of Isis** (protection in all circumstances).

***Ba*** - Represented as a human-headed bird, **Ba**, the soul of the deceased, is a kind of spirit that leaves the body at death and goes wandering as he likes: **Ba** can stay in the tomb near the body, go into the funerary chapel to appreciate the offerings or, can even wander around to find the favorite walks of the deceased.

***Book of the Dead*** - Appearing from the New Kingdom on, this collection of texts, more correctly called the "**Book for Going Out by Day**", is a loose group of recipes that are supposed to secure the revival of the deceased in the afterworld, giving him complete freedom in his movement and giving him everything he needs in the underworld. The chapters, very often decorated with illustrations and vignettes, are written on a papyrus scroll, put into the coffin or inserted in the linen wrappings of the mummy. Many copies of this funerary book have been found, but they are all different, some have chapters that do not exist in others. To this day, there have been 190 different chapters recorded; they are numbered from I to CXC.

***Canopic jars*** - The mummified viscera of the deceased are preserved in four canopic jars, made out of alabaster or limestone, and put under the protection of four gods, called the ***four sons of Horus***, and four goddesses. ***Hapy***, with a baboon's head, and ***Nephthys*** watch over the lungs; ***Imset***, with a man's head, and ***Isis*** watch over the liver; ***Qebehsenuf***, with a falcon's head, and ***Serket*** watch over the intestines; ***Duamutef***, with a jackal's head, and ***Neith*** watch over the stomach.

***Cartouche*** - This word designates the elongated buckle symbolizing the universal reign of the king, and encircling the fourth and fifth names of the pharaohs: the **Throne name** (or **He of the Sedge and the Bee**) and the **Birth name** (or **Son of Re'**).

***Coffin Texts*** - As opposed to the "**Pyramid texts**", only reserved to the royal person, these funerary texts are used by civilians and decorate the coffins during the Middle Kingdom. Issued from the democratisation of the funerary creeds, they allow the deceased to identify himself to ***Osiris*** in the afterworld, through spells and recipes aimed to deify the deads.

***Consort*** - This word is used to qualify a goddess who is considered to be the wife of a god in a sanctuary. In the **Theban** triad, the goddess ***Mut*** is the consort of the ***Amun,*** in the **Memphite** triad, the goddess ***Sakhmet*** is the consort of the ***Ptah*** and in the **Elephantine** triad, the goddess ***Satis*** is the consort of ***Khnum***.

***Cosmogony*** - It is a mythic tale describing the creation of the world and the settling of the natural elements of the universe: earth, sky, stars... Many religious centers have their own cosmogonic legend: **Heliopolis**, **Memphis**, **Esna**, **Thebes**, **Crocodilopolis**, **Hermopolis**... Each one has a creative god, called "demiurge," who conceives his creation with his own means; for example,it is said that ***Ptah*** creates "by his thought and his tongue" and ***Khnum*** shapes the gods, the human beings and the objects on his potter's wheel.

***Cosmography*** - On the walls of the tombs, there are scenes that show the world as it was believed to be by the ancient Egyptians. They present the topography of the Nile Valley or the underworld. In the **Valley of the Kings**, some tombs offer some very complete cosmographies, that are assembled in the funerary books: the "**Book of Doors**" and the "**Book of What is in the Tuat**".

***Crown*** - Most of the deities wear crowns that make them identifiable. Without the headdress, they are sometimes very difficult to distinguish: ***Osiris*** wears the **atef** crown, a high crown with two feathers; ***Horus*** wears the **pshent**, which is the double crown of Lower and Upper Egypt; ***Isis*** wears a throne, sign used to write her name; ***Ma'at*** and ***Shu*** wear an ostrich feather; ***Serket*** wears the corpse of a scorpion... and so on for each deity of the pantheon.

***Demiurge*** - This term designates the creative god in a cosmogonic system: ***Re'*** in **Heliopolis**, ***Sobek*** in **Crocodilopolis**, ***Ptah*** in **Memphis**, ***Khnum*** or ***Neith*** in **Esna**, ***Amun*** in **Thebes**...

***Dromos*** - The Greeks gave this name to the alley that extends the axis of a temple, towards the outside, to link it to another one or to a landing on the Nile. These alleys are often bordered with sphinxes or recumbent lions.

***Embalment*** - There is a very precise logic behind the invention and use of the techniques for mummification. In Egypt, death is not the end, but a passage to another form of existence. But, this passage is very dangerous because during the period of dying, the different elements of the human personality (the **ka**, the **ba**, the name, the body, the heart...) separate, each one keeping its own integrity. If they can all be gathered together, a second life is possible; and so, everything is done to preserve the body, since if it is damaged, all chance of another life fades away. The embalming has to preserve the body. The technique consists in taking the entrails out of the body, before putting it in a bath of natron for seventy days to dehydrate it. The body is washed afterwards, perfumed, and wrapped in linen, with inserted amulets. The viscera are mummified apart and kept in the four **canopic jars** protected by the **four Sons of Horus** (***Imset***, ***Duamutef***, ***Qebehsenuf*** and ***Hapy***).

***Ennead*** - In the beginning, an Ennead designates a group of nine primeval gods who together symbolize the whole set of elementary forces of the universe, as in for instance, the cosmogony of **Heliopolis**. Later the word **Ennead** loses its etymological meaning in designating the divine assembly that is at the source of a theological system whatever the number of gods within it. So, in **Abydos**, there are seven gods in the Ennead, and fifteen in **Thebes**.

***Spirit*** - The Egyptians call "spirit" all the beings who in the underworld make the path to the kingdom of the dead difficult and perilous. They are powers of chaos, hybrid animals, inferior beings and malevolent forces. They are often armed with lances and knives to attack the deceased. There are hundreds of them on the walls of the tombs, but it is possible to make them powerless by knowing their names or the right formula to say in case they are encountered. This is why their representation is always accompanied by a very detailed legend that gives the deceased all the information allowing him never to be caught unaware.

***Hieracocephalic*** - This term is used to designate any divinity that appears in the guise of a hawk. The most famous falcon god of the Egyptian pantheon is ***Horus***; this is why the Greeks baptized his town **Hierakonpolis**.

***Hypogeum*** - This word designates a tomb, either royal or civilian, dug into a cliff.

***Ka*** - This notion is difficult to understand for there is no concept in our language for the Egyptian **ka**. It is considered to be a manifestation of the life force, either conservative or creative, that continues to live after the death of the body. Offerings and funerary formulas are addressed to the **ka**, which is the element allowing the deceased to survive in the afterworld.

***Legend of Osiris*** - It is the most famous legend of Egyptian literature. Unfortunately, only the Greek writer **Plutarch** gives a complete version of this story in his *De Iside a Osiride*. The Egyptian texts are very mutilated and have many gaps. This legend of Heliopolitan tradition recalls the three periods in the life of the gods from the great Ennead: the murder of ***Osiris*** by ***Seth***, the birth and childhood of ***Horus*** and the struggle between ***Horus*** and ***Seth*** for the kingdom of earth.

***Naos*** - It has two meanings: the stone tabernacle in which the statute of the god was placed, as well as the enclosed shrine areas that were reserved for statues in ancient Egyptian temples.

***Nome*** - It is the name given by the Greeks to the administrative regions of the Nile valley. The number, names and territorial limits of the nomes changed constantly during thirty centuries of Egypt's history, according to the social and political reforms. But whatever the period, the nome remains an economical and fiscal entity, each with its own temples, gods and laws, which must be respected.

***Psychostasis*** - This Greek word means "the weighing of the soul," and refers to the chapter CXXV of the "**Book of the Dead**," when the deceased is introduced by ***Anubis*** to the judgment hall, and his heart is put on one side of the scales. ***Ma'at***, the symbol of righteousness, on the other. This weighing, watched by ***Thoth***, is to determine whether the deceased is worthy to enter the realms of ***Osiris***. The "***Great Eater***," a monstruous hybrid being, stays by the scales, ready to claim its victims in case of an unfavorable judgment.

***Pyramid Texts*** - They are the funerary texts engraved on the walls of the pyramids built at the end of the Old Kingdom. The oldest text goes back to the time of *Unas,* the last king of the 5th dynasty. All the kings of the 6th dynasty had them inscribed, but they disappear with the unrest of the First Intermediate Period. Magical spells, different hymns and religious incantations are supposed to secure the king immortality and to allow him to unite with the sun.

***Royal Titulary*** - They are the five names taken by the pharaoh upon ascending the throne. I: the **Horus name** (I) - II: the **Nebti name** (or **He of the Two Ladies**) - III: the **Golden Horus name** - IV: the **Throne name** (or **He of the Sedge and the Bee**) - V: the **Birth name** (or **Son of Re'**).

***Sacred animals*** - The Egyptians think that any animal is the receptacle of a part of the divine power, whether good or bad. This explains the large number of cults of sacred animals: the crocodile (god ***Sobek***), the ibis or the baboon (god ***Thoth***), the cat (goddess ***Bastet***), the bull (god ***Apis***), the falcon (god ***Horus***), and the jackal (god ***Anubis***) are the main ones.

***Scepters*** - These attributes, held by gods, kings and noblemen, determine the qualities and functions of those who carries them. The most common divine scepters are the following: the **heka** scepter (crook) and the **flail** for the god ***Osiris***, the **wadj** scepter (rod as a stalk of papyrus) for the feminine deities, and the **was** scepter (a long stick with a canine head) for the masculine deities.

***Sema-tawi*** - This Egyptian term is translated as *"to unite the Two Lands."* It is symbolized by two emblematic plants: the lotus of Upper Egypt and the papyrus of Lower Egypt, entwined around a trachea by two deities, ***Horus*** and ***Seth***, or two gods ***Ha'py***. This trachea in hieroglyphic writing means "to unite". The **sema-tawi** represents the union between the South and the North in one kingdom.

***Serekh*** - It is a rectangle representing the front of a palace, topped by the symbol of a hawk or falcon, in which the first name of the king was inscribed: the **Horus name**.

***Sphinx*** - This lion with a human head, called the sphinx, is in general the symbol of the king or a sun god. As the incarnation of the king, it is supposed to fight against enemies and to protect good men. As representative of the sun god on earth, it watches over the western regions, into which the deceased and the sun leave. The sphinx of **Giza** belongs to this second category of sphinxes: it incarnates ***Harmakhis***, "***Horus*** on the Horizon" and ***Hurun***, the god from **Canaan** assimilated into ***Harmakhis*** from the New Kingdom.

***Stela*** - It is a monolithic slab, usually of limestone, on which can be engraved different inscriptions: decrees, official announcements, funerary formulas, lists of offerings. Sometimes these stelae are memorials. They are votive offerings that the faithful put into the sanctuaries, after having made a pilgrimage to a holy place, or to thank the god of a temple for having made a wish come true.

***Triad*** - It is a group of three deities of the same town, in a family structure: god, goddess, god son or goddess daughter. The most famous triads are the triad of **Memphis** with ***Ptah***, ***Sakhmet*** and ***Nefertem***, the triad of **Thebes** with ***Amun***, ***Mut*** and ***Khons***, the triad of **Elephantine** with ***Khnum***, ***Satis*** and ***Anukis*** and the triad of **Abydos** with ***Osiris***, ***Isis*** and ***Horus***.

***Tuat*** - It is the Egyptian word that designates the underworld that is to say the afterworld.

***Universal Master*** - In myths and legends, the creative god of the Heliopolitan cosmogony is designated as the "Universal Master." In fact, this is the sun god, and is can also be called ***Atum***, ***Khepri*** or ***Re'***, ***Re'-Atum-Khepri***, ***Re'-Atum*** or ***Atum-Khepri***.

***Uraeus*** - This word designates the cobra with the extended hood, the eye of ***Re'*** of the Heliopolitan legend, topping the royal headdress. It is said that he protects the king everywhere under any circumstances *"even during the night when he sleeps"*, and he repels all the enemies of Pharaoh.

***Ushabti (Shabti*** or ***Shawabti)*** - Put in the tomb, this mummiform figurine has, in the underworld, to do all the daily tasks for the deceased. A few words are carved on them: *"O Ushabti! If X (the deceased) is required to do one of the tasks in the next world... You will say: Here I am!"* Appearing during the Middle Kingdom, the **ushabties** are made, according to the status of the deceased, of wood, bronze, faience, stone or terra-cotta. Sometimes there are hundreds of them in the same tomb.

***Writing*** - The Egyptians have used three main forms of writing: a sacred writing, the **hieroglyphic**, remarkable for the delicacy of its drawings, and two civil writings, much simpler, the **hieratic** taken over by the **demotic** as far back as the 7th century B.C.

# CHRONOLOGY

## *Early Dynastic Period*
## *3150-2686 B.C.*

**1st Dynasty**
- Narmer
- Aha
- Djer
- Djet
- Den
- Semerkhet
- Qa'a

**2nd Dynasty**
- Hetepsekhemwy
- Raneb
- Nynetjer
- Peribsen
- Khasekhemwy

## *Old Kingdom*
## *2686-2181 B.C.*

**3rd Dynasty**
- Sanakht
- Djoser
- Sekhemket
- Khaba
- Huni

**4th Dynasty**
- Sneferu
- Khufu
- Djedefra
- Khephren
- Menkaure
- Shepseskaf

**5th Dynasty**
- Userkaf
- Sahura
- Neferirkara-Kakai
- Shepsaskara
- Raneferef
- Nyuserra
- Menkauhor
- Djedkara
- Unas

**6th Dynasty**
- Teti
- Pepy I
- Merenra
- Pepy II

## *First Intermediate Period*
## *2181 - 2060 B.C.*

**7th Dynasty** *(totally unknown)*

**8th Dynasty** *(from Memphis)*
- Wadjkara
- Kakara Ibi

**9th and 10th Dynasties** *(from Herakleopolis)*
- Khety I
- Merykara
- Neferkara
- Khety II

**11th Dynasty** *(Theban and contemporary with the end of the 10th Dynasty)*
- Mentuhotpe I
- Intef I
- Intef II
- Intef III

## *Middle Kingdom*
## *2 060 - 1 782 B.C.*

**11th Dynasty**
- Mentuhotpe II
- Mentuhotpe III
- Mentuhotpe IV

**12th Dynasty**
- Amenemhet I
- Senusret I
- Amenemhet II
- Senwuret II
- Senwuret III
- Amenemhet III
- Amenemhet IV
- Sobekneferu

## *Second Intermediate Period*
## *1782 - 1570 B.C.*

**13th Dynasty** *(a dynasty during which the kings, who are native Egyptians, still seem to reign over the two kingdoms of Egypt, the capital of which is in Iti-Tawi, in the oasis of el-Faiyum)*
- Wegaf
- Intef IV
- Hor
- Sebekhotpe II
- Khendjer
- Sebekhotpe III
- Neferhotpe I
- Sebekhotpe IV
- Aya
- Neferhotpe II

**14th Dynasty** *(contemporary with the end of the 13th dynasty, which ends in an obscure fashion; the 14th Dynasty only reigns over the eastern part of the Delta)*
- Nehesy

**15th and 16th Dynasties** *(Hyksos dynasties: these kings, coming from the East, take power in Egypt and set up their capital in Avaris)*
- Sharek
- Yakub-Har
- Khyan
- Apepi I
- Apepi II
- Anather
- Yakobaam

**17th Dynasty** *(Theban Dynasty, who tried to win back the land by driving out the Hyksos)*
- Sebekemsaf II
- Intef VII
- Taa I
- Taa II
- Kamose

## *New Kingdom*
## *1570 - 1070 B. C.*

**18th Dynasty** Ahmose
Amenhotep I
Tuthmosis I
Tuthmosis II
Hatshepsut
Tuthmosis III
Amenhotep II
Tuthmosis IV
Amenhotep III
Amenhotep IV-Akhenaten
Smenkhkara
Tutankhamun
Ay
Horemheb

**19th Dynasty** Ramesses I
Sethos I
Ramesses II
Merneptah
Amenmessu
Sethos II
Siptah
Tausret

**20th Dynasty** Sethnakhte
Ramesses III
Ramesses IV-Ramesses XI

## *Third Intermediate Period*
## *1070 - 656 B. C.*

**21st Dynasty** *(two contemporary kingdoms: the priest kings usurp the power and reign in Thebes over Upper Egypt, whereas in the Delta, Smendes proclaims himself king at the death of Ramesses XI, sets up his capital in Tanis and reigns over Lower Egypt)*

| **Tanis** | **Thebes** |
|---|---|
| Smendes I | Herihor |
| Amenemnisu | Piankh |
| Psusennes I | Pinedjem I |
| Amenemope | Masaharta |
| Osorkon the Elder | Menkheperre' |
| Siamun | Smendes II |
| Psusennes II | Pinedjem II |

**22nd Dynasty** *(Lybian dynasty, coming from Bubastis and reigning in Tanis)*
Sheshonq I
Osorkon I
Sheshonq II
Takelot I
Osorkon II
Takelot II
Sheshonq III
Pimay
Sheshonq V
Osorkon IV
Harsiesis

**23rd Dynasty** *(contemporary with the end of the 22nd Dynasty, the first ruling in the Delta over Lower Egypt, and the second ruling in Leontopolis over Middle Egypt)*
Pedubastis I
Sheshonq IV
Osorkon III
Takelot III
Rudamon
Iuput

**24th Dynasty** *(first Dynasty of Sais)*
Tefnakht
Bocchoris

**25th Dynasty** *(from Nubia: the kings of Napata take over the rule in Egypt)*
Piy
Shabaqo
Shabitqo
Taharqo
Tanutamani

## *Late Period*
## *664 - 332 B.C.*

**26th Dynasty** *(second Dynasty of Sais)*
Psamtek I
Nekau
Psamtek II
Apries
Ahmose
Psamtek III

**27th Dynasty** *(first Persian rule)*
Cambyses
Darius I
Xerxes
Artaxerxes I
Darius II
Artaxerxes II

**28th Dynasty** Amyrtaios

**29th Dynasty** Nepherites I
Hakor

**30th Dynasty** Nectanebo I
Teos
Nectanebo II

**31st Dynasty** *(second Persian rule)*
Artaxerxes III
Arses
Darius III Codoman

**332-323 B.C.** *In 332 B.C., Alexander the Great enters into Egypt and frees the country of the Persian rule by chasing Darius III away. At his death in 323, Egypt passes under the government of one of his lieutenants, Ptolemy, who takes the title of pharaoh in 305 and founds the Ptolemaic dynasty.*

**305-30 B.C. - Ptolemaic Dynasty**
Ptolemy I Soter I
Ptolemy II Philadelphus
Ptolemy III Euergetes I
Ptolemy IV Philopator
Ptolemy V Epiphanes
Ptolemy VI Philometor
Ptolemy VII Neos Philopator
Ptolemy VIII Euergetes II
Ptolemy IX Soter II
Ptolemy X Alexander I
Ptolemy XI Alexander II
Ptolemy XII Neos Dionysos
Ptolemy XIII and Cleopatra VII
Ptolemy XIV and Cleopatra VII
Cleopatra VII

**30 B.C. - 395 A.D. - Roman Egypt**

# HIEROGLYPHS

Three classes of signs need to be distinguished in hieroglyphic writing: the **phonograms**, the **logograms** and the **determinatives**.

9/10ths of the system are **phonograms** which have a sound value and can be divided into three groups: *uniconsonantal* signs (one sign has the value of a consonant or semi-consonant), *biconsonantal* signs (one sign has the value of two consonants or semi-consonants) or *triconsonantal* signs (one sign has the value of three consonants or semi-consonants). The *biconsonantal* and *triconsonantal* signs are accompanied by one or several *uniconsonantal* signs, the *phonetic complements*, used to reinforce the phonetic value of the signs they go with.

The **logograms** represent a concept and allow a word to be noted through an individual sign whose meaning is broadly equivalent to its appearance (a boat for "boat").

The **determinatives** are not pronounced but qualify the word which precedes them; they are put behind the word they determine.

Before deciphering a text in hieroglyphs, the translator must give a phonetic value to the signs. This preliminary task of ***transliteration*** is absolutely necessary to be able to pronounce the Egyptian words. But the hieroglyphic writing, just as its transliteration, only uses consonants or semi-consonants which makes the proper pronounciation impossible to establish. So, to be able to pronounce the words, one must add vowels between the consonants or transform semi-consonants into vowels.

Egyptian language can be written from top to bottom, right to left or left to right (what we use for convenience), never from bottom to top. The sense of reading is indicated by the signs representing animals or people; if they look at the left, we read from left to right, and vice versa. In the inscriptions, signs are situated in a harmonious more than in a logical way. The scribe works gathering and situating the signs, which can be vertical, horizontal or square, according to their shape.

## *Uniconsonantal signs*

**Vulture**
Pronunciation: **a**
Transliteration: *3*

**Owl**
Pronunciation: **m**
Transliteration: ***m***

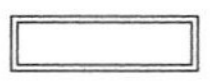

**Pool**
Pronunciation: **ch**
Transliteration: *š*

**Reed in flower**
Pronunciation: **i**
Transliteration: *i*

**Dash of water** or **crown**
Pronunciation: **n**
Transliteration: ***n***

**Hill slope**
Pronunciation: **k**
Transliteration: *ḳ*

**Double reed in flower**
Pronunciation: **y**
Transliteration: *y*

**Mouth**
Pronunciation: **r**
Transliteration: ***r***

**Basket with handle**
Pronunciation: **k**
Transliteration: ***k***

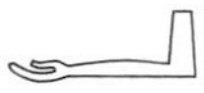

**Forearm**
Pronunciation: **a**
Transliteration: ᶜ

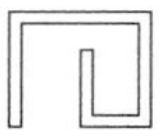

**Building plan**
Pronunciation: **h**
Transliteration: ***h***

**Jar support**
Pronunciation: **g** (hard)
Transliteration: ***g***

**Quail chick**
Pronunciation: **ou**
Transliteration: ***w***

**Wick of linen**
Pronunciation: **h** emphatic
Transliteration: ***ḥ***

**Loaf of bread**
Pronunciation: **t**
Transliteration: ***t***

**Leg**
Pronunciation: **b**
Transliteration: ***b***

**Placenta (?)**
Pronunciation: **kh** (jota)
Transliteration: ***ḫ***

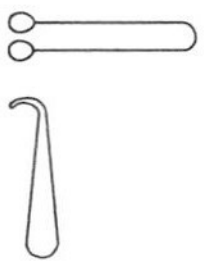

**Rope or pestle**
Pronunciation: **tch**
Transliteration: ***ṯ***

**Seat**
Pronunciation: **p**
Transliteration: ***p***

**Cow vulva (?)**
Pronunciation: **ç**
Transliteration: ***h***

**Hand**
Pronunciation: **d**
Transliteration: ***d***

**Horned viper**
Pronunciation: **f**
Transliteration: *f*

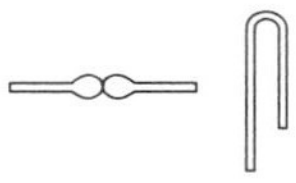

**Bolt** or **linen**
Pronunciation: **s** (muffled)
Transliteration: *s*

**Cobra**
Pronunciation: **dj**
Transliteration: ***ḏ***

# *A few biconsonantal signs*

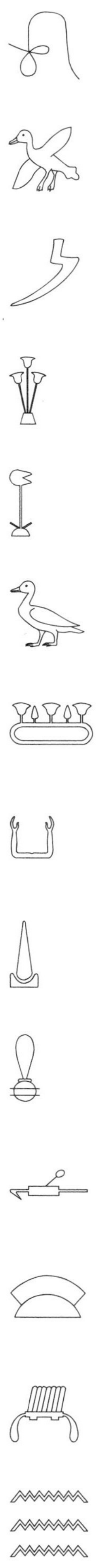

**Coiled lasso**
Pronunciation: **wa**
Transliteration: ***wa***

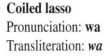

**Bird in flight**
Pronunciation: **pa**
Transliteration: ***p3***

**Scythe**
Pronunciation: **ma**
Transliteration: ***m3***

**Bouquet of Papyrus**
Pronunciation: **ha**
Transliteration: ***ḥ3***

**Lotus flower**
Pronunciation: **kha**
Transliteration: ***ḫ3***

**Duck**
Pronunciation: **sa**
Transliteration: ***s3***

**Flooded field, marshes**
Pronunciation: **cha**
Transliteration: ***š3***

**Lifted arms**
Pronunciation: **ka**
Transliteration: ***k3***

**Tool for fire**
Pronunciation: **dja**
Transliteration: ***ḏ3***

**Vase in a net**
Pronunciation: **mi**
Transliteration: ***mi***

**Harpoon**
Pronunciation: **wa**
Transliteration: $w^{c}$

**Sun behind a hill**
Pronunciation: **kha**
Transliteration: ***ḫ***$^{c}$

**Animal's thorax**
Pronunciation: **au**
Transliteration: ***3w***

**Three streams of water**
Pronunciation: **mu**
Transliteration: ***mw***

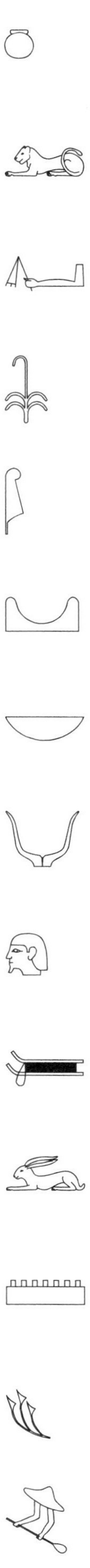

**Vase**
Pronunciation: **nu**
Transliteration: ***nw***

**Recumbent lion**
Pronunciation: **ru**
Transliteration: ***rw***

**Hand holding a flail**
Pronunciation: **khu**
Transliteration: ***ḫw***

**Stalk and leaf**
Pronunciation: **sou**
Transliteration: ***sw***

**Ostrich feather**
Pronunciation: **chu**
Transliteration: ***šw***

**Double mountain**
Pronunciation: **dju**
Transliteration: ***ḏw***

**Basket**
Pronunciation: **neb**
Transliteration: ***nb***

**Cow horns**
Pronunciation: **up**
Transliteration: ***wp***

**Face seen from the side**
Pronunciation: **tep**
Transliteration: ***tp***

**Sled**
Pronunciation: **toum**
Transliteration: ***tm***

**Rabbit**
Pronunciation: **oun**
Transliteration: ***wn***

**Checkerboard**
Pronunciation: **men**
Transliteration: ***mn***

**Tuft of grass**
Pronunciation: **hen**
Transliteration: ***ḥn***

**Two arms rowing**
Pronunciation: **çen**
Transliteration: ***ẖn***

**Pointed arrow**
Pronunciation: **sen**
Transliteration: ***sn***

**Human eye**
Pronunciation: **ir**
Transliteration: ***ir***

**Little bird**
Pronunciation: **our**
Transliteration: ***wr***

**Plan of a house**
Pronunciation: **per**
Transliteration: ***pr***

**Hoe**
Pronunciation: **mer**
Transliteration: ***mr***

**Face seen from the front**
Pronunciation: **her**
Transliteration: ***ḥr***

**Bunch of linen stalks**
Pronunciation: **djer**
Transliteration: ***ḏr***

**Knotted fox skins**
Pronunciation: **mes**
Transliteration: ***ms***

**Libation vase**
Pronunciation: **hes**
Transliteration: ***ḥs***

**Looped string**
Pronunciation: **ches**
Transliteration: ***šs***

**Vulture**
Pronunciation: **met/mut**
Transliteration: ***mt/mwt***

**Skin pierced with an arrow**
Pronunciation: **set**
Transliteration: ***st***

**Throne**
Pronunciation: **set**
Transliteration: ***st***

**Everlasting Pillar**
Pronunciation: **djed**
Transliteration: ***ḏd***

# A few triconsonantal signs

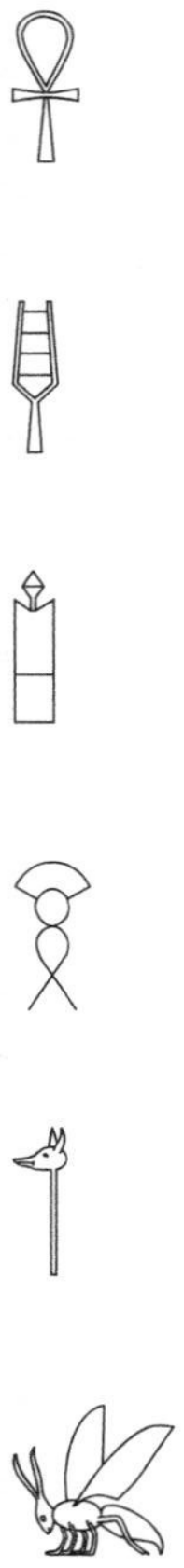

**Sign of life**
Pronunciation: **ankh**
Transliteration: ***ꜥnḫ***

**Mast**
Pronunciation: **aha**
Transliteration: ***ꜥḥꜥ***

**Column, pillar**
Pronunciation: **ioun**
Transliteration: ***iwn***

**Broom**
Pronunciation: **wah**
Transliteration: ***w3ḥ***

**Jackal-headed scepter**
Pronunciation: **usir**
Transliteration: ***wsr***

**Bee**
Pronunciation: **bit**
Transliteration: ***bit***

**Heart and trachea**
Pronunciation: **nefer**
Transliteration: ***nfr***

**Stick wrapped in cloth**
Pronunciation: **netcher**
Transliteration: ***nṯr***

**Carob shell**
Pronunciation: **nedjem**
Transliteration: ***nḏm***

**Palm branch**
Pronunciation: **renep**
Transliteration: ***rnp***

**Bread on a mat**
Pronunciation: **hetep**
Transliteration: ***ḥtp***

**Stalk of a papyrus**
Pronunciation: **wadj**
Transliteration: ***w3ḏ***

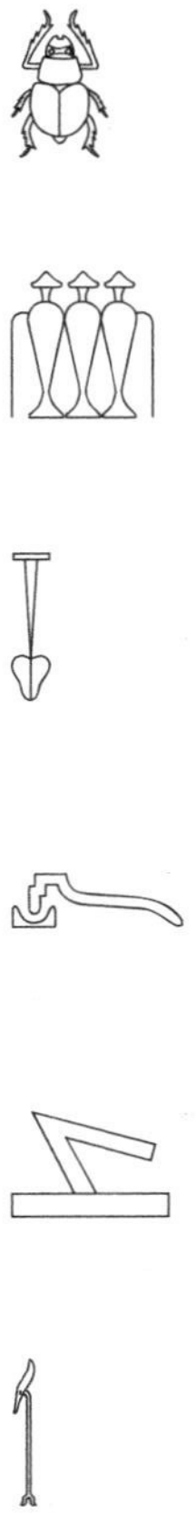

**Scarab**
Pronunciation: **khéper**
Transliteration: ***ḫpr***

**Three libation vases**
Pronunciation: **khenet**
Transliteration: ***ḫnt***

**Lungs**
Pronunciation: **sema**
Transliteration: ***sm3***

**Ax on a block**
Pronunciation: **setep**
Transliteration: ***stp***

**Trap**
Pronunciation: **guereg**
Transliteration: ***grg***

**Scepter of the gods**
Pronunciation: **was**
Transliteration: ***w3s***

# A few determinatives

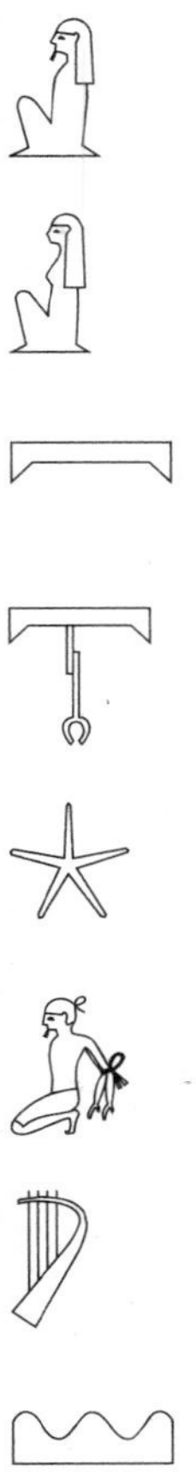

**Man sitting**
Male deities

**Woman sitting**
Female deities

**Stylized celestial vault**
Sky and cosmos

**Sky and lightning**
Night and darkness

**Star**
Stars and constellations

**Prisoner**
Enemy, rebel and foreigner

**Harp**
String instrument and harp

**Mountain**
Deserts and foreign lands

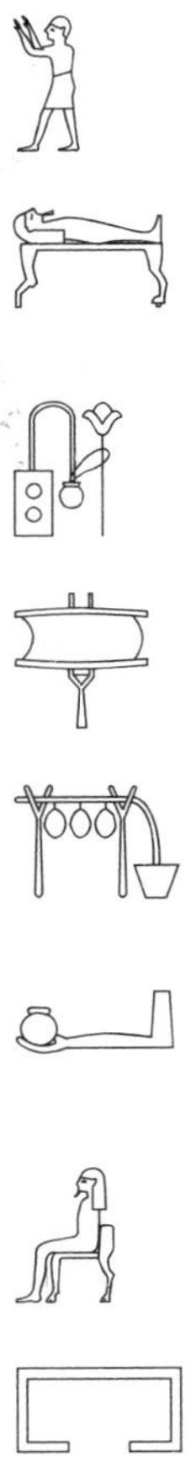

**Man worshipping**
Prayer and worship

**Mummy on funerary bed**
substantives linked to death

**Scribe's palette**
Scribe and writing

**Sail of a boat**
Air, breath and sailing

**Vine-trellis**
Vine, wine, fruit and orchard

**Arm carrying a vase**
Offering and gift

**Sitting dignitary**
To be noble and venerable

**Plan of a house**
Houses and buildings

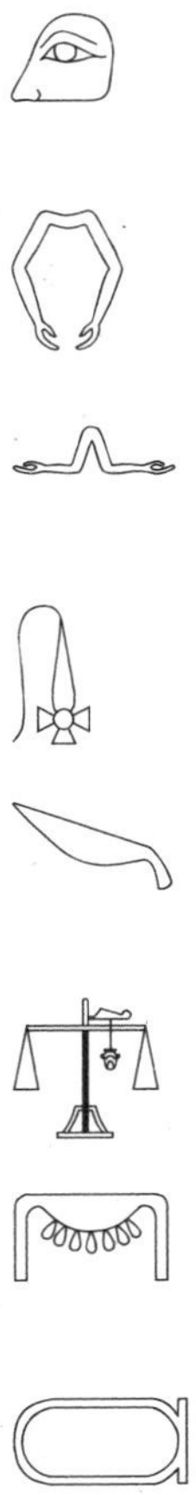

**Nose and face**
Nose, smell and joy

**Two joined arms**
To embrace and wrap

**Two outstretched arms**
Negation and negative things

**Brazier**
Fire, heat and cooking

**Knife**
Knife, cutting and slicing

**Scales**
scales, weighing

**Symbol of gold**
Precious metal

**Cartouche**
Royal name and king

# BIBLIOGRAPHY


**Cyril Aldred**,
*The Egyptians*, Thames and Hudson, London / New York, 1961 / 1984

**John Baines et Jaromir Malek**,
*Atlas of Ancient Egypt*, Andromeda, Oxford, 1980 and 1996

**Paul Barguet**,
*Le Livre des Morts des Anciens Égyptiens - Les Textes des Sarcophages des Égyptiens du Moyen Empire* (two volumes),
Cerf, Littérature Ancienne du Proche Orient (LAPO), 1967 and 1986

**Maria Carmela Betró**,
*Hiéroglyphes, les mystères de l'écriture,* Flammarion, 1995

**Peter A. Clayton**,
*Chronicle of the Pharaohs*,
Thames and Hudson, London, 1994 and 1999

**Marc Collier and Bill Manley**,
*How to read Egyptian hieroglyphs*,
British Museum Press, London, 1998 and 1999

**Christiane Desroches-Noblecourt**,
*Toutankhamon, vie et mort d'un pharaon*, Pygmalion, 1988

**Christiane Desroches-Noblecourt**,
*Amours et fureur de la Lointaine*, Stock, Paris, 1995

**Mircea Eliade**,
*Traité d'histoire des religions,* Payot, Paris, 1987

**Raymond O. Faulkner**,
*The Ancient Egyptian Book of the Dead*,
under the management of C. Andrews, London, 1985 and 1996

**Raymond O. Faulkner**,
*The Ancient Egyptian Pyramid Texts* (two volumes), Oxford, 1969

**Henri Frankfort**,
*Ancient Egyptian Religion*, New York, 1948

**Sir Allan Gardiner**,
*Egypt of the Pharaohs*, Oxford / New York, 1961

**John Gwyn Griffiths**,
*The conflict of Horus and Seth from Egyptian and Classical sources*,
Liverpool, 1960

**John Gwyn Griffiths**,
*Plutarch's De Iside et Osiride*, Swansea, 1970

**Nicolas Grimal**,
*Histoire de l'Égypte ancienne*, Fayard, 1988

**George Hart**,
*Egyptian myths*, British Museum Press

**Herodotus**,
*Histories, Book II,* A. B. Lloyd,
Herodotus Book II.1: an intoduction (Leiden, 1975)
Herodotus Book II.2: commentary 1-98 (Leiden, 1976)
Herodotus Book II.2: commentary 99-182 (Leiden, 1988)

**Erik Hornung**,
*Der Eine und die Vielen*, Darmstadt, 1971

**Claire Lalouette**,
*Textes sacrés et textes profanes de l'Ancienne Égypte,*
Connaissances de l'Orient, Gallimard UNESCO, Paris, 1984

**Claire Lalouette**,
*Au royaume d'Égypte - Thèbes ou la naissance d'un empire - L'empire des Ramsès* (three volumes),
New edition, Collection Champs, Flammarion, 1995

**Mark Lehner**,
*The complete Pyramids*, Thames and Hudson, London

**Dimitri Meeks et Christine Favard-Meeks**,
*La vie quotidienne des dieux égyptiens*, Hachette, 1993

**Siegfried Morenz**,
*Osiris und Amun, Kult und Heilige Stätten*, Munich, 1966

**Georges Posener, Serge Sauneron et Jean Yoyotte**,
*Dictionnaire de la civilisation égyptienne*, Hazan, 1959

**Donald B. Redford**,
*Akhénaton, the heretic king*, Princeton, 1995

**Nicholas Reeves**,
*The complete Tutankhamun*, Thames and Hudson, London, 1990

**Nicholas Reeves and Richard H. Wilkinson**,
*The complete Valley of the Kings*, Thames and Hudson, London

**Serge Sauneron et Jean Yoyotte**,
*La naissance du monde selon l'Égypte ancienne*,
Sources Orientales I, Seuil, Paris, 1959

**Ian Shaw et Paul Nicholson**,
*British Museum, Dictionary of Ancient Egypt*,
British Museum Press, 1995

**Jacques Vandier**,
*Manuel d'archéologie égyptienne* (six volumes de texte et deux volumes de planches), Éditions A. et J. Picard & Cie, Paris, 1952 à 1964

**Jacques Vandier**,
*La religion égyptienne*, Paris, P.U.F., Collection "Mana", 1949

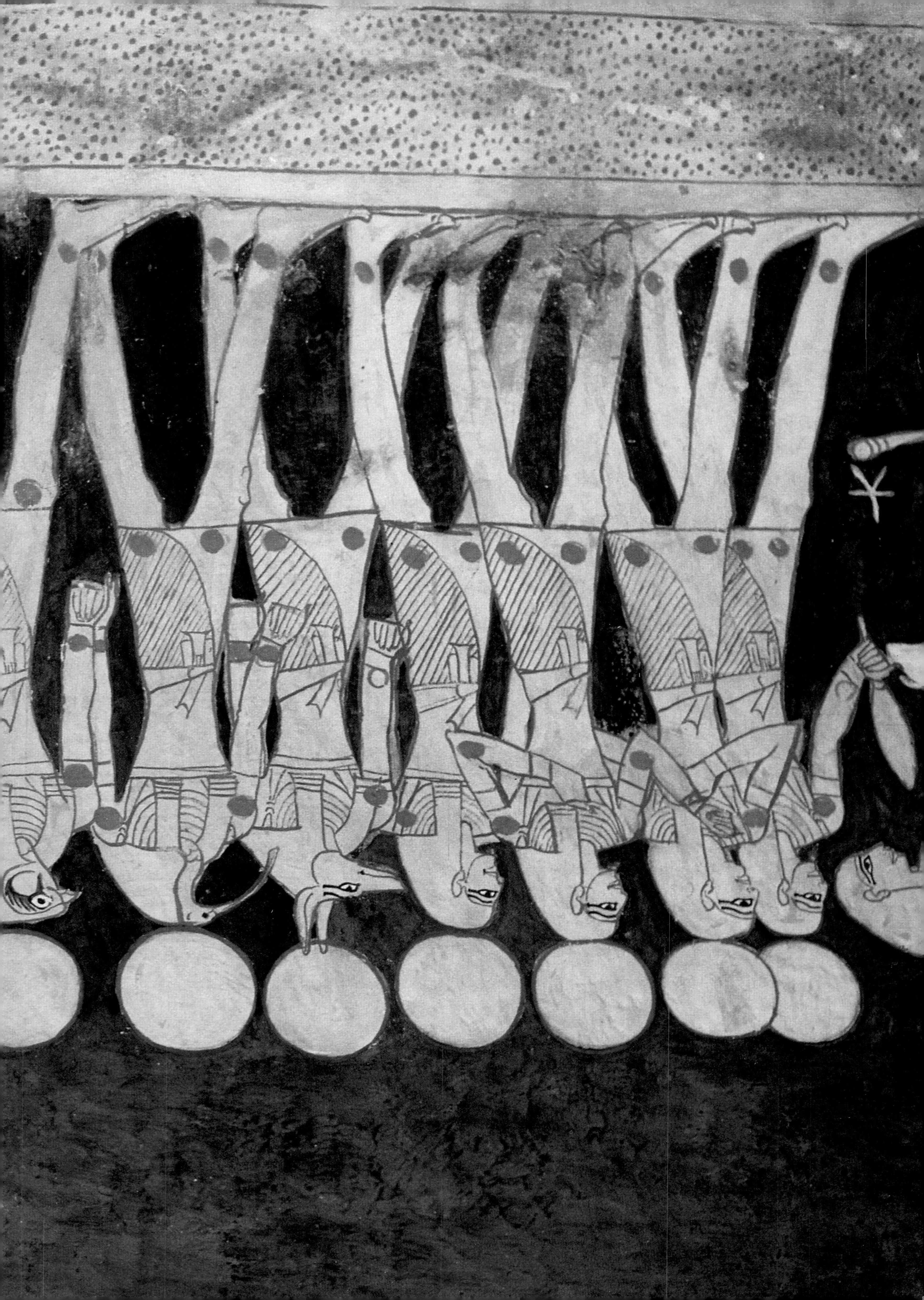